ART IN LAW

Nicholas Hasluck

Connor Court Publishing

Published in 2019 by Connor Court Publishing Pty Ltd

Connor Court Publishing Pty Ltd
PO Box 7257
Redland Bay QLD 4165
sales@connorcourt.com
www.connorcourtpublishing.com.au
Phone 0497-900-685

Printed in Australia

ISBN 978-1-925826-56-2

To Sally Anne

About the Author

Nicholas Hasluck was born in Canberra. He studied law at the University of Western Australia, then Oxford, before practising law in Perth. He served as a Judge of the Supreme Court of Western Australia, Chair of the Literature Board, the Commonwealth Writers Prize and the Art Gallery of Western Australia. His many novels include *The Bellarmine Jug*, winner of The Age Book of the Year Award.

Acknowledgments

Art in Native Title was presented to a UWA Law Faculty conference on Art in Law, July 2017. Three pieces were first published in *Quadrant* as follows: *Bacon, Hobbes and the Integrity of Conservatism*, July/August 2018; *The Merchant of Venice and Other Victims,* December 2018, *Sounds of Division from Uluru,* July/August 2019. *Cervantes in Law* was first published in *Brief* (WA Law Society), December 2018.

Other Books by Nicholas Hasluck

Novels
Quarantine
The Blue Guitar
The Hand That Feeds You
The Bellarmine Jug
Truant State
The Country Without Music
The Blosseville File
A Grain of Truth
Our Man K
Arbella's Baby
Dismissal
Rooms in the City
The Bradshaw Case

Short Stories
The Hat on the Letter O
Wobbling the Whiteboard

Essays and Memoirs
Collage
Offcuts from a Legal Literary Life
Light That Time Has Made (Ed)
The Chance of Politics (Ed)
The Legal Labyrinth
Somewhere in the Atlas
Legal Limits
The Hasluck Banner
Jigsaw: Patterns in Law and Literature

Poetry
Anchor and Other Poems
On the Edge
Chinese Journey
A Dream Divided

CONTENTS

1

ART IN NATIVE TITLE

A work of art will often reflect the response of its creator to the revelations of daily life. In the visual arts the creative work usually reflects what can be seen or touched. A literary work will be inclined to cast light on ways of living or some human dilemma. Art can also be a source of knowledge about things we have never seen, or even imagined. It may persuade us to look at the world in a fresh light.

Skilfully crafted stories about the law, in plays or movies or works of fiction, can be used to reveal truths or insights that may lead to a deeper understanding of the legal system, as the pieces in this book will seek to show.

The ebb and flow of the story in a work of fiction encourages the reader to dwell upon different ways of looking at a situation, not for the purpose of reaching a final judgment, as in a court of law, but simply as a means of reviewing various possibilities from standpoints other than one's own. Ruminations of this kind, nurtured by imaginative works, may well encourage readers within the legal system to think creatively, to act fairly, and to consider possibilities that the law in its current form may have been inclined to exclude or suppress.

Let me underpin my theme by turning to a novel I brought out not so long ago: *The Bradshaw Case*.[1] This work of fiction takes the reader to some controversial issues about the origin of rock art in the Kimberley region of Western Australia. It looks at the handling of native title claims in the aftermath of the High Court's contentious ruling in the case now known as *Mabo*. It underlines my earlier observations, for the novel is a way of talking freely about certain standpoints in postmodern times that are sometimes said to cause 'offence'. It illustrates the wisdom in theatre of old: give a man a mask and he will tell the truth.

In *The Bradshaw Case* the tale is told by a fictitious young lawyer called Colin Everett, a newcomer to the Kimberley, who is drawn into a fierce dispute about native title being heard in a seedy courthouse at Broome. The disappearance of a key witness on the eve of trial points to threats of blackmail, or even worse. To win the case for the Aboriginal claimants, Colin and his fellow lawyers have to find the witness, get the better of their opponents, and probe the origin of rock art situated on the so-called Ngerika peninsula.

The reader learns that a mining company is keen

---

1   Hasluck N *The Bradshaw Case* (Australian Scholarly Publishing/ Arcadia, 2016)

to get its hands on an iron ore body in the claim area. Success or failure will depend on evidence drawn from the writings of the 19th century explorer Joseph Bradshaw and later research by an anthropologist called Jack Otway who has been close to the Ngerika claimants for many years. Much will depend also upon what is said by an elderly Aboriginal man, Tracker Ningulai, who has an intimate knowledge of the land affected by the claim and knows what happened on some of the recent expeditions.

The case ends in a swirl of controversy. The story offers a poignant glimpse of how the future can be shaped by half-truths and human failings, and by contested versions of the past. In the words of the anthropologist in question: 'People want to see the past put to use.'

What facts and real events frame the story? Since the High Court's decision in the 1992 *Mabo* case and the enactment of related legislation, it has been open to Aboriginal litigants to make claims for native title based on a long connection to the land in question and evidence of ancestral practices, including rock art. Claims are resolved in courts and outdoor sittings in real places such as Broome or other towns in the Kimberley.

There is also another layer of fact in *The Bradshaw Case,* an account of early exploration which some readers may not be entirely familiar with, but which will gradually be made clear to them by the inexperienced narrator, Colin Everett, for he is on a learning curve too.

The reader learns from Everett and other lawyers involved in the case that Bradshaw – a real person – refers to Joseph Bradshaw, described early on as 'an explorer, adventurer and fellow of the Royal Geographical Society.'

On the first page of the novel, as a preface to all that follows, the reader is provided with a short excerpt from the diary of Joseph Bradshaw of 16 April 1891 – a diary that does indeed exist – to this effect: '*In the afternoon Fred and I rode out and found that the river at this place emerges through a gorge in the sandstone range and forms a large rocky pool. Further on there was a great pile of rocks on the far side of the river. In the secluded chasms of these rocks were numerous Aboriginal paintings which appeared to be of great antiquity.*'[2]

Colin Everett finds out in due course that in the years after Bradshaw's discovery there were various expeditions to the Kimberley in which anthropologists sought to record and document the diverse customs and forms of rock art in the region. The reader learns that as to the various images found in caves and sandstone shelters there were two principal forms of art.

The first to be discovered were the Wandjina images chanced upon by Lieutenant George Grey in 1838.

---

2   Bradshaw, J. Journal of Joseph Bradshaw from January 31st 1891 to June 6th 1891, Mitchell Library B967, Microfilm copy held by Battye Library, Acc 1271A.

Typically, the head of each figure is surmounted by a halo of bright red rays, beneath which appears a face painted vividly white, with the eyes thick blobs of black, but no mouth or chin.

The second form, being images of an entirely different kind, were those discovered by Joseph Bradshaw 30 years later, at the end of the 19th century: that is, the paintings described in Bradshaw's diary as appearing to be of 'great antiquity'. His opinion was shared by the anthropologists who followed him. They characterised the slim, ornate figures represented in the explorer's sketches (and on the cover of the novel) as being many thousands of years older than the Wandjina art.

The unique form of the Bradshaw art has engendered controversy from the time of its first discovery to the present day, for no one can speak definitively as to where it came from.

In addition to the passage I quoted a moment ago Bradshaw's 1891 diary contains a later passage as follows: *'I do not attribute these drawings to the present representatives of the black race. .... Some of the human figures were life-size, the bodies and limbs very attenuated and represented as having numerous tassel-shaped adornments appended to the hair, neck, waist, arms and legs; but the most remarkable fact in connection with these drawings is that wherever a profile face is shown the features are of a more pronounced aquiline type, quite different from those of any natives we encountered. Indeed, looking at some of the groups, one might think himself viewing the walls of an ancient Egyptian temple.*[3]

One of the anthropologists who followed Joseph Bradshaw was Professor A.P Elkin from the University of Sydney. In 1930, after field work in the region, Elkin said that there were certain images in the Kimberley which seemed to owe their origin to 'external influence, if not agency.' He added: *'This would seem to be the case with the strange paintings found in a cave along the Prince Regent River by Bradshaw.'*[4]

This brings me to a passage from a book written by a leading Australian anthropologist, the late Grahame Walsh.[5] *'Agnes Schulz the highly-skilled chief artist accompanying the 1938 Frobenius Institute Expedition worked under adverse conditions on site to complete many large scale copies of art panels … (She) made lengthy trips by mule to visit the widely separated sites, at times travelling with the Aboriginal guides …. The now accepted term 'Bradshaw paintings' seems to have been first introduced in the published works of Frau Agnes Schulz, largely due to the absence of any Aboriginal name or term by which they could be referenced.'*

Thirty years after the research undertaken by Agnes Schulz from the Frobenius Institute, a widely-respected anthropologist from the West Australian Museum, Ian Crawford, drawing upon fieldwork from five expeditions

3   Bradshaw, J (supra). See also Proceedings of Kimberley Society 27 March 2010 p. 127.

4   Elkin, A.P: *Rock Paintings of North West Australia, Oceania* Vol 1 No 3 December 1930, p. 258.

5   Walsh, G *Bradshaw Art of the Kimberley* (Takarakka Nowan Kas Publications, 2000) p. 14.

in the 1960s, summed up in this way: *'Although Wandjina paintings are impressive because of their massiveness, size and their colour, they lack finesse and movement. In complete contrast are the 'Bradshaw' figures, small red paintings which show people busy dancing and hunting .... The origin of these paintings presents a mystery ... Unlike the majority of the paintings in the Kimberley, the Bradshaw figures are of no importance to the Aborigines, who simply regard them as the work of a bird. What man they say would bother to paint the pictures: such a man would gain no prestige for wasting his time in this way. The paintings are 'rubbish paintings' illustrating nothing of interest or value. This attitude is in marked contrast to the respect paid to the Wandjina and the paintings which are associated with myths and songs.'* [6]

The anthropologist I mentioned earlier, the late Grahame Walsh, having studied the works of Bradshaw, Elkin, Schulz and Crawford, and pursuant to his own findings in the field, formed the view that the Bradshaw images had not been created by Aboriginal artists but were the work of an earlier or different race.

Walsh's findings were said to verify the view expressed by Billy King, an elder of the Kupungarri Aboriginal Community in the West Kimberly: *'I think what the old people told me is true, they were done by different people to us, not from any of our tribes, maybe long before we existed.'* [7]

There is, of course, a wide range of other books and

---

6   Crawford, I.M, *The Art of the Wandjina* (Oxford University Press, 1968) p. 81.

7   Walsh, G (supra) p. 425.

opinions about these matters, many of them (especially since native title was introduced in the 1990s) directed to refuting the view held by the late Grahame Walsh. Steps have been taken to put dates on the two forms of rock art, but no final conclusions have been reached. There seems to be a loose or informal consensus that the Wandjina art could be up to 5000 years old, but the Bradshaw images probably first came into existence about 17,000 years ago.

A number of recent works draw attention to an aspect of the matter that Ian Crawford touched upon; that is, some Aboriginal groups in the Kimberley see the paintings as the work of a bird: a small bird known as 'Gwion Gwion'. The term Gwion Gwion is increasingly being used by tourist guides and others to describe the paintings, although I see from my last visit to the National Museum in Canberra that the works are still being described by the museum curators as 'Bradshaw' images.

I have probably said enough to show the nature of the ongoing controversy concerning the origin of the Bradshaw art, and to give prospective readers of *The Bradshaw Case* a sense of what the novel is about – the struggle for control of the purported Ngerika peninsula, and of its past. As in many courtroom dramas, real or imagined, where the twists and turns of the plot depend upon disputed facts and the production or suppression of crucial exhibits, the evidence in the Bradshaw case is open to various interpretations.

It was this feature of the situation – the ambiguity of the evidence in actuality – plus a long-standing interest in anthropological issues that aroused my interest in the Bradshaw controversy some years ago. Since then I have been to the Kimberley many times, by road, boat and helicopter, and have examined rock art paintings, both Wandjina and Bradshaw, in many remote places. In the end, for the reasons I mentioned at the outset, I was inclined to acquaint readers of goodwill with my quest for an understanding of the Bradshaw art by way of a work of fiction, bearing in mind that there have been many books about the mystery written by specialists.

Needless to say, I am not qualified to offer a final judgment, or even a firm opinion, about the nature of the anthropological contest at the heart of my novel. What the characters say and do is for readers to ponder. A novel of this kind is simply a way of encouraging people, students and would-be lawyers in particular, to keep an open mind about controversial matters in the course of reaching their own conclusions.

I hold firmly to the view – a view doubted in some quarters – that any person with an interest in the pre-history of Australia and the heritage of humankind should feel free to talk about an intriguing issue of this kind, an issue about the origin of the so-called Bradshaw or Gwion Gwion art that the anthropologist Ian Crawford, over fifty years ago, characterised as 'a mystery.' It is only by looking into the mysteries around us that we can arrive at what we need to know. Indeed, as one of the characters in the novel is heard to say towards the end of the book: '*If truth is a value it is principally because it is true, not because it takes courage to say it aloud, although that is important.*'[8]

The nature of the contest and some subsidiary issues in *The Bradshaw Case* can be illustrated by turning to a passage in the novel in which Jack Otway, the elderly anthropologist, is being cross-examined by counsel for the State of Western Australia.

'*You call the images in question Bradshaw art?*'

'*I do. As did my father, and most of the anthropologists who came after him. That was the name given to them by the German expeditions in the late 1930s. They were named after Joseph Bradshaw who was the first to discover images of that kind.*'

'*And you say further that they were so named because the local people had no interest in them, and no name for them?*'

Jack hesitated. '*There is a good deal of contemporary evidence to that effect, but there could be other explanations.*'

'*Your father was of the opinion that there was a lack of interest because the images were created many thousands of years ago by a different race?*'

'*That was his opinion.*'

'*And you have always held the same opinion?*'

Jack took a deep breath and sat quite still. '*That is true,*' *he conceded, bringing the silence to an end.* '*I hold that opinion. As do a number of others. It is certainly a matter that has to be*

---

8   Hasluck N (supra) p. 211.

investigated. In a scientific way, that is.'

'So on your view of the matter, even if the panel of rock art be treated as evidence of human habitation, the island subject to the claim was never inhabited by a race of people from which the Ngerika claimants are descended?'

Jack closed his eyes and grimaced, as if trying to make sense of the question. 'That is for the court to decide, or so I am told.'

These issues are then pursued by the presiding judge who, in response to the pleadings, has insisted that the rock art in question be called Gwion Gwion: the Aboriginal name for a local bird.

Justice Saypol put down his pen. 'Your opinion about an earlier and different race seems very bold,' he said.

Jack shrugged. 'Not to me. It is an opinion I have held for many years. Throughout my adult life, in fact. Which means I am not inclined to abandon it too easily.'

'I hear what you say. But the law generally looks to what can be seen or touched. Tangible evidence. It is wary of opinions. Even from experts who claim to know what they're talking about.'

'I understand, your Honour. That has been explained to me. But if asked I must surely be entitled to express my opinion. Especially when it bears upon the history of the place in question, and the matters in issue.'

'In a case like this, the law provides the test of what is in issue, and the law is above us all.'

'With respect, your Honour, research and the pursuit of scientific truth are even higher. They have always gone wherever

they wish to go.'

'Not in my court. We are bound by the statute and the rules of evidence. They are the rules I intend to apply. The court in this case isn't interested in unsubstantiated opinions or fanciful theories. It is interested in ancestral practices on Dumont Island and the Ngerika peninsula. The heritage of the various language groups. The link between one phase and the next.'

'The heritage of the language groups!' Jack agreed. 'Of course! But I am interested also in the heritage of humankind. How far back it goes, and what lies behind the twists and turns that followed. In the Kimberley region rock art is the key to it. As it was in the caves of Lascaux in France. As it was for Galileo when his telescope revealed a vast new sky, previously invisible to the naked eye. So I am not to be prised loose too easily from the opinion I have held for so long. The Bradshaw paintings are the work of an earlier race. They are the way in to a greater understanding of human creativity.'

The bespectacled Judge, his bookkeeper's face unimpressed by what was being dumped in his tray, came back at the witness sharply. 'Way in or way out? One way or another we seem to be losing our bearings with all this high-flown talk.'

He picked up his pen and leaned forward. 'Let us come to the point. You seem to be in favour of the claimants' case, but for some reason I don't quite understand you won't say that the panel of rock art on Dumont Island was created by their ancestors. I am beginning to wonder how much time we can spend on all this theorising. I must have evidence upon which to base a finding. Tangible evidence. Without it I will be left with no option but to dismiss the claim. And that would be very disappointing to all those who have laboured so hard to bring this case to court.'

The judge checked his notes before adding a further thought. 'And let me remind you that the art we are speaking of is called Gwion Gwion. I would like to hear more about that and less about Joseph Bradshaw. In the end, his so-called "discovery" is probably incidental to what matters most. The claim to country and a way forward for those who think of it as their homeland.'

'I am with your Honour in that regard, but the fact remains that the term Gwion Gwion is of comparatively recent origin. The reasoning behind my opinion starts with Bradshaw, and the ornate human figures he discovered, which are completely unlike all the other forms of rock art. His name appears in all the writings on this subject and I fear we will become confused if his name is simply wiped out.'

'Mr Otway. I have done what I can to be reasonable, but I sense that you are trying to draw me in. You are seeking to commit the court to another round of abstruse discussion about matters of interest to you, but of little relevance to the main point. I have to tell you frankly, I won't have it.' The judge pointed his pen at the witness. 'It is often better all round if a person holding a strong opinion, especially an opinion that might strike some as slightly odd, can see his way clear to take account of the realities around him, and re-examine his position accordingly. Do you follow what I say?'

The Judge glanced at his notes again. 'I have some evidence from you concerning ways of life and practices on the peninsula, but no evidence I can act on concerning the offshore islands. And to some extent, I have to say, your evidence about the mainland is clouded by certain doubts I am beginning to have about your *general credibility …. So please just plain get on with it, and tell us what you know about Wandjina and Gwion Gwion art and the ancestral practices of the various language groups. Do I make myself clear?'*

Jack was clearly affronted by these remarks. He seized the rail of the witness box. 'I am surely entitled to my opinion? To speak the truth as I see it?'

'The court will decide what the truth is, and once that decision is made, that will be the truth!'

'But there are so many queries to be dealt with about this art! Can we really assume that these ornate human figures, with their tassels and sashes and headdresses, spread throughout the sandstone outcrops of the Kimberley, were created by a small bird with a beak dipped in blood? Is it no longer possible to ask such a question?'

'You are challenging what people have come to believe,' the Judge snapped. 'Do you go so far as to challenge matters of faith?

'I do. As Galileo did. And as Charles Darwin did many years later. And I challenge also the pretence that the language groups likely to be affected by any ruling made by the court — named absurdly "groups A, B and C" — have the common features attributed to them. A proper respect for the realities of this region demands that crude generalisations of such a kind be resisted.'

This was greeted with an icy judicial glare. 'Let me ask you again. Do you persist in this fanciful notion that the Kimberley was once inhabited by an earlier and different race?'

'That has been my opinion throughout my adult life and I hold

it still. One has only to look at the Bradshaw figures to know that they come from somewhere beyond our present understanding. Far back.'

The Judge came smartly to his feet and bowed abruptly. 'The court will stand adjourned for a short period.'

What are we to make of exchanges of this kind between judge and witness? From the trial of Socrates to the ordeal of the elderly anthropologist in *The Bradshaw Case*, law has frequently found its way into literature as a means of casting light upon various political controversies, moral dilemmas and legal issues. A court of law becomes a theatre in which events enacted in the grip of rage or passion are reconstructed in order to round off the plot or to wrap up the author's critique of the legal system.[9]

Documents and testimony in a court can establish the facts but they can't always recapture the mood nurturing the matter in contention. Playwrights and novelists, by reproducing gossip in the barrack rooms and back streets, may sometimes provide a more vivid picture of what went on in the corridors of power at a crucial moment, a more convincing explanation as to why an empire collapsed, or an apparently stable society was brought to the brink of ruin, than appears in the report of a Royal Commission or an official history.

It follows from these observations that it will be useful for advocates and others in the legal system to

---

9   Shapiro F and Garry J (Ed), *Trial and Error* (Oxford University Press, 1998) p. vii.

take account of literary techniques in presenting a case or a point of view. Substantive law may vary from place to place but a need for procedural fairness is common to most widely respected legal systems.[10] The notion that a party should be heard in regard to any contentious issue brings with it, by necessary implication, a requirement that the party's story should be well-presented. Advocates should have a clear understanding of how stories are constructed and expressed.

The use of literature and other forms of art in getting to grips with the workings of the law is important. It is a different but creative way of reviewing issues that bear upon the pursuit of justice. Legal practitioners and would-be lawyers should be encouraged to consider diverse interpretations of the materials before them and to ponder a wide range of possibilities, so that the ideals of the law and related remedies can be fully achieved. In one of Patrick White's novels a character respected for his powers of insight is heard to say: there are other worlds but they are with us in this one. A critique of the law, enhanced by imagination, will lead to an improved vision of society.

---

10   Hampshire S, *Justice is Conflict* (Duckworth, 1999) p. 18.

2

BIAS IN THE MERCHANT OF VENICE

The trial scene in Shakespeare's play *The Merchant of Venice* can be used to explore some current issues concerning the rules of natural justice and claims to special rights and privileges. In contemporary times, when the 'identity' of a complainant or an alleged victim seems to be increasingly important, there is much to ponder in the fate of Shylock, the notorious Venetian money-lender at the centre of the trial scene, who looked to the law to enforce a contractual penalty – the yielding up of a pound of flesh – but was eventually subjected to a draconian penalty himself: an unexpected outcome and a useful reminder of some enduring questions about the workings of the law.

Should legal rules be strictly enforced or should there always be room for equity or moderation? What is justice and to what extent, if any, must allowance be made for mercy, a quality in which Shylock, as a Jew, was supposedly deficient? In this case, who was the victim in the end – the debtor who faced death if his bond was enforced, or the Jewish creditor who was brought down in due course by a dodgy trial process and a law against aliens? Or were the ultimate victims those members of the general public whose livelihoods might well be affected if it became known that the trial was tainted by corruption?

I will return to some general issues of this kind, but first let me set out certain features of the plot bearing upon the trial scene in question. As in most trials, the prospects of the parties shift in the course of the Venetian proceedings and this brings with it a continuing need for reassessment of liability and degrees of guilt, before and after the verdict, especially in a play where no allowance is made for appeal.

Antonio, a Venetian merchant, has well-laden ships at sea but in the meantime he needs money to help his friend Bassanio woo the heiress, Portia. He borrows money from Shylock, a Jewish money-lender, who has been treated harshly by Antonio and his compatriots on other occasions and harbours deep-rooted (but carefully concealed) resentments accordingly.

In what is described by Shylock as a piece of 'merry sport', something not to be taken too seriously, the loan agreement, in lieu of interest, includes a grisly penalty – if Antonio fails to repay the loan on time, Shylock is entitled to cut out a pound of flesh 'in what part of your body pleaseth me.'

Antonio's ships don't come in on time and the repayment date passes. Spurning repayment several times over, Shylock sues for specific performance. He wants his pound of flesh. He brings his case before a court constituted by the Duke of Venice.

The Duke voices an unfavourable opinion of the Jewish money-lender as a man incapable of pity, but then reveals that he has sent for Bellario, a learned lawyer in Padua, to 'determine' the dispute. In the meantime, Portia has decided to assist her husband's friend by disguising herself as a distinguished Doctor of Laws. She presents the Duke with a letter of commendation from Bellario and in that way, pursuant to what is in effect a delegation (or perhaps a gradual usurpation) of the Duke's judicial power, she becomes the presiding judge. She is certainly treated as such by the parties.

Early on, when Shylock insists, again and again, that 'I'll have my bond', Antonio seems to accept that strict compliance with the agreement cannot be denied 'for the commodity that strangers have with us in Venice, if it be denied, will much impeach the justice of the state' and 'the trade and profit of the city.' In other words, in the language of our own era, the parties recognise the problem of sovereign risk. Foreign investment in Venice will be threatened if its courts are seen to be unpredictable or partial.

Portia, in her role as putative judge, seeks to moderate a literal reading of the contract by urging the jewish money-lender to be merciful, for the quality of mercy 'droppeth as the gentle rain from heaven' and 'blesses him that gives, and him that takes.'

Shylock is unmoved by her eloquent plea. He will have his bond. And even Portia seems to accept that for the sake of commercial certainty, and to avert sovereign risk, contracts must be strictly enforced. She notes, reluctantly, that if an established decree be altered it will be 'recorded for a precedent, and many an error by the same example will rush into the state.' She then concludes that Shylock is entitled to enforce the bond. She says: 'The law allows it and the court awards it.'

This early tilt towards Shylock lulls him into a false sense of security. 'Most rightful judge!' he exclaims. But this exclamation simply sets the scene for the dramatic reversal that follows. 'Tarry a little,' Portia says to Shylock, 'There is something else. The law hath yet another hold on you.'

The imposter judge then embarks upon a piece of sophistry that leads to Antonio's release from the bond. He is excused because the money-lender is not entitled to shed any blood in enforcing the bond.

To hold, as Portia does, that Shylock may take a pound of flesh but no blood is patently absurd, for the bond must have implicitly authorised what was necessary for Shylock to get his pound of flesh. Moreover, Portia's legalistic and hyper-technical 'flesh-but-no-blood' construction of the contract is probably unnecessary because there are alternative rationales for denying Shylock's suit.

She could have questioned whether the bond was binding in the first place because it seems that Antonio was induced to sign it pursuant to a misrepresentation that it was simply a 'merry sport.' Alternatively, she could have relied upon the various offers of repayment which were spurned by Shylock because offers of this kind will usually be sufficient to justify relief against forfeiture or to avert the risk of specific performance. She could have relied upon public policy that weighs against the enforcement of draconian penalties. It might even be said that this was the true basis of her decision in favour of Antonio to set aside the bond.

But now, having been denied enforcement of his bond, worse was to follow for Shylock. Portia, the imposter judge, invokes a notorious Aliens statute; that is, if it be proved against an alien that he seeks the life of any citizen 'the party against which he doth contrive shall seize one half of his goods, the other half comes to the privy coffers of the state, and the offender's life lies in the mercy of the Duke.' Shylock is then virtually compelled by the masquerading trial judge to convert to Christianity or die.

Portia wraps up the proceedings by ordering the Clerk to draw up a deed of gift. Shylock, soon to be deprived of his means of livelihood and all his assets, crushed by what has happened – the legal proceedings that seemed to start so well – finishes up in what seems to be a state of forlorn bewilderment. 'I pray you,' he says, 'give me leave to go from hence; I am not well, send the deed after me, and I will sign it.'

That is the last the audience will see or hear of Shylock.

Some loose ends are then tied up as the play draws to a close. Still in disguise, but in a playful mood, Portia tests the loyalty of her husband by some toing and froing over the whereabouts of her husband's wedding ring. When she resumes her true identity the loving couple are reunited: whereupon the husband's friend, Antonio, seals the happy ending with these words: 'Sweet lady, you have given me life and liberty, for here I read for certain that my ships are safely come to road.'

The sense of goodwill all round that accompanies the final curtain, and Portia's eloquence in describing the 'quality of mercy' in the course of the trial scene, undoubtedly leaves a favourable impression of the fair lady in question. For many playgoers she arguably personifies the spirit of equity and humane resourcefulness.

In other words, by a skilful disguise and related stratagems, she rescues her husband's friend Antonio from the clutches of the merciless Jewish money-lender. Her speeches in court seem to reflect a sensible recognition that strict rules of law, however necessary to stabilise commercial transactions and underpin a well-ordered society, must be applied with tact and sensitivity so that the equitable spirit of the law is not sacrificed unnecessarily to the strict letter.

Her stance seems to recognise that the evolution of a legal system is often and perhaps typically from strict and simple rules to more flexible standards. Her actions may also convey to the more discerning eyes of experienced or even would-be advocates that, in the end, succinct points of interpretation may prove to be more effective in securing a desired outcome than lofty (and possibly sentimental) rhetoric about abstract concepts such as mercy.

Nonetheless, before proceeding too far down this track, the path of uncritical admiration, let us return to Shylock's ignominious departure from the court, the scene in which he slinks off to await arrival of the deed he is now obliged to sign. As often happens with losing parties, the initial mood of bewildered disappointment may begin to fester and soon turn into an acute sense of injustice, especially on the facts set before us in this play.

When the verdict is reduced to its simplest form, it amounts to this: no pound of flesh, no repayment of the amount borrowed by Antonio, but on the contrary, forfeiture of Shylock's property, and his forced conversion to the Christian faith.

In other words, after what seemed to Shylock to be a promising start to the trial, Shylock's case for strict enforcement of the bond is shoved aside by what is arguably a piece of unconvincing sophistry – Portia's 'flesh-but-no-blood' ruling. Worse, Shylock is then, in effect, suddenly convicted of an offence confined to aliens of which he was given no prior warning and no real opportunity to answer the charge. He is forced to abandon his fundamental beliefs in order to avert the risk of execution. All of this has been brought about by a woman without any legal training who is not only fraudulently posing as a judge but has a clear conflict of interest because she is so friendly to one of the parties that she is determined to do whatever it takes to rescue him.

It would almost certainly be thought by a litigant in Shylock's position, as he reviews the trial with the benefit of hindsight, that the entire proceedings, and indeed the communal values reflected in the process, were heavily weighted against him from the outset. The word 'jew' is constantly used as an epithet and the supposed superiority of the Christian faith is arguably implicit in the outcome, for he is forced to abandon his beliefs. So, upon further reflection, who was the victim in the circumstances presented to the audience? Who was the victim in the end?

As I indicated early on, works of literature can act as very useful pointers to important features of the legal system. For centuries the traditional symbol of justice has been a blindfolded woman holding in one hand a balance scale and in the other a sword. Justice wears a blindfold, we are usually told, so she cannot show favouritism or yield to bias or prejudice. Thus, if justice does not see the parties before her, then in weighing the evidence she cannot prefer the strong over the weak, friends over enemies, rich over poor, neighbours over strangers, one sex over another.

In theory, the law is supposed to treat all equally, without fear or favour, and the blindfold on the symbol of justice is designed to help ensure such equal treatment. Shylock presumed that his case was being evaluated by a judge of that description. Along the way, he refers to the youthful but apparently learned Doctor of Laws before him – Portia in disguise – as 'a worthy judge', 'a rightful judge' and 'a well-deserving pillar of the law.' To understand the feelings that are bound to have tormented him when the crushing verdict was handed down, depriving him of his goods and even his deepest beliefs, one must begin by taking a closer look at what is meant by the sense of injustice.

What usually passes for injustice is an act or verdict that goes against some known or legal or ethical rule. On that view of the matter only a victim whose position doesn't match the rule-governed prohibition can be said to have suffered an injustice. On the other hand, if the rule fits the facts, then any complaint about the outcome of the case can probably be characterised as the victim's subjective reaction: a misfortune perhaps, but not an injustice.

If a properly constituted but overly legalistic court had ruled in favour of strict compliance with the bond, thus putting Antonio's life at risk, a sense of injustice particular to he and his supporters would surely be valid. As I have indicated, apart from Portia's specious 'flesh-but-no-blood' argument, there were various persuasive grounds in law and equity, for holding that the bond should not be enforced – it was induced by a misrepresentation, rules of specific performance and public policy negate the infliction of a draconian penalty, especially where offers of full payment have been made.

Likewise, Shylock's presumed sense of injustice would surely be validated in circumstances where various rules of natural justice were infringed. He was given no forewarning of the charge brought against him and the issue was determined by an untrained and biased judge.

The model of injustice I have just described has been the commonly accepted one; that is, the usual rules have not been complied with and a party has suffered loss. But the apparent lack of justice being done because the rule doesn't fit will not necessarily cover all cases in which a sense of injustice arises.

A person who is the victim not so much of a broken rule but of disappointed expectations or reprehensible conduct, in circumstances where communal values would ordinarily point to a more acceptable outcome, may also harbour a sense of injustice. In a vibrant democracy grievances of this kind will increasingly be voiced as certain sections of the public contend that what are arguably legitimate claims have been overlooked. It then becomes far more difficult to identify those who are properly characterised as victims, people to whom remedies *should* be granted, and those who have simply experienced misfortune.

On the facts of the Venetian trial supposedly before us, and if the more obvious breaches of particular rules mentioned earlier are removed from the equation, would it have been open to Antonio to claim it was unjust to have his life put at risk because of some facetious repartee at the time the contract was made which left him thinking that the special bond was just 'a merry sport'? Would it be open to Shylock, apart from all else, to complain of Portia's rank hypocrisy when she exhorted him to be merciful but proved to be unmerciful herself when the balance tilted against him?

In both of these scenarios the disappointed expectations of the claimant would not be based on the breach of a legal rule but on a belief that people should act with decency. If communal standards cease to reflect the notion of decency, due to widespread corruption or a blind pursuit of self-interest, will trade and commerce begin to suffer? One may also ask, as I did at the outset, whether, in the circumstances depicted in the play, the Venetian community as a whole was the real victim of the trial process, a dodgy hearing corrupted by the presence of an untrained and biased judge? Who would do business in such a place if these flaws in the process became widely known?

There is arguably another question to be addressed, a matter which gives the play a particular contemporary relevance in an Australian setting. We are living in what the art critic Robert Hughes once called 'a culture of complaint.' It is becoming increasingly common for complainants to seek relief in the courts or through the media upon the basis that they are victims of discriminatory conduct. The events complained of might not amount to a crime but the person affected might be left with a sense of injustice if nothing can be done about it. Section 18C of the *Racial Discrimination Act 1975* (Cwth), for example, provides for relief where a person feels offended by a discriminatory or hostile act referable to race or ethnic origin. Provisions of this kind point to a need to look carefully at what can be said to constitute an injustice in contemporary times. They point also to some other questions.

Should Shakespeare's play, *The Merchant of Venice*, which has been performed in public for several centuries, continue to be performed? It might be characterised by some members of a contemporary audience as a play reeking of prejudice against Shylock's race and Jewish origin. They may claim to be offended or insulted by what is said and done to Shylock. Section 18C of the Racial Discrimination Act which seeks to prohibit questionable conduct could be a vehicle for such a claim.

One likes to think that such a claim would be unenforceable. In this, as in so many of his plays, Shakespeare is dramatizing a wide variety of human traits and thereby casting light on universal themes. He does so without necessarily pursuing a particular cause or point of view, for his knowledge of human nature seems boundless and his intention benign. One is simply left with a variety of viewpoints and much to ponder. The play forces the audience to think about the workings of the legal system and the way trials should be conducted. For that very reason, like many other works of literature, it will be of use to would-be lawyers and legal practitioners alike as they dwell upon the nature of human rights and what underlies the sense of injustice. If that be so, how could one think of banning such a play?

With these thoughts in mind I must note in passing that the prohibition against offensive or insulting speech in section 18C of the Racial Discrimination Act is presently qualified by section 18D which provides an exemption in respect of artistic works, a proviso which may well be sufficient to protect producers of the *Merchant of Venice* in most cases. It seems obvious to many jurists, however, that freedom of thought, and the right to talk freely about the issues thrown up by a play of this kind, would be better served by a decisive abolition of the prohibition contained in section 18C because it limits freedom of speech.

For the time being, let me simply confirm that trial scenes have frequently been used in literature as a vehicle for showing the way in which human beings deal with a vast array of moral, psychological and political issues including the question of what arouses the sense of injustice. A trial scene, as in *The Merchant of Venice,* can dramatize such issues in a way that renders them compelling.

This brings me to the question of whether it is appropriate to critique a trial process established in earlier times by giving weight to rules of natural justice applicable today. Improved procedural rules would probably have altered the outcome. On the other hand, however, Shakespeare's rhetoric suggests that it will always be difficult to counter underlying attitudes that favour a desired result. Can a disciplinary tribunal on a university campus that condones the banning or abuse of scholars from Israel, for example, be trusted to deal fairly with a party to the proceedings of Jewish descent? In the event of an appeal, can one safely assume in contemporary times that a court will stick to applying settled law to established facts and not be distracted by ongoing debate about the status of a Jewish nation in the Middle East?

These are significant questions. Many lawyers in Australia, and even some judges, with fixed views about the past, especially as to matters of Aboriginal dispossession, have been increasingly inclined in recent years to look for facts, or what are said to be flaws in official practices, that confirm beliefs they have already formed. They read the past backwards from the present, excluding matters that may prove inconvenient, such as the scarcity of resources in earlier times or a felt need to take remedial action in cases of neglect.

In *Mabo,* for example, it is not entirely surprising that Justices Deane and Gaudron struck an apologetic note in characterising their 'unusually emotive language' as necessary to override certain long-standing rules of real property that might otherwise have been treated as decisive. They seemed to acknowledge that they were about to push beyond the pale in order to achieve what seemed to them to be an enlightened outcome. How do tendencies of this kind bear upon the need for judicial impartiality?

These ruminations bring me back to my opening remarks. Shakespearean plays and other memorable works of literature can be used to cast light on the law in action and the meaning of justice. They can provide an extra dimension to what is taught.

Would-be lawyers go to law school not so much to acquire knowledge that seems relevant to resolving legal issues, but for certain skills – for the habit of attention, for the lawyer's way of entering quickly into another person's thoughts, for the art of expression, for the capacity to say what clients can't say for themselves, for the technique of indicating assent or dissent in graduated terms and for the ability to work out what is possible within a given time. Weight must also be given to the need for moral courage and compassion as appears in what Portia put to Shylock about the legalistic stance that led to his downfall: *Though justice be thy plea, consider this. That, in the course of justice, none of us should see salvation: we do pray for mercy.*

It follows from these observations that would-be lawyers must be reminded by their teachers from time to time that the intuition of an artist can be of use in practising law. With that in mind, let me close by recalling what was put to Shylock's daughter by her lover in the final act of *The Merchant of Venice*: *The man that hath no music in himself / Nor is not moved with concord of sweet sounds / Is fit for treasons, stratagems and spoils / The motions of his spirit are dull as night.*

Astute lawyers will not only be attuned to the needs of their clients but also to the underlying realities of the matter in hand. They must know how to read between the lines and respond to the sounds of hidden music until, in Portia's words: *The crow doth sing as sweetly as the lark.*

3

TRUTH IN HOBBES AND BACON

Works of fiction are mercurial. They can be shaped to suit the author's mood, or the mood of a bygone era can be shaped to suit the author's purpose. A play or novel set in Shakespearean times, for example, can nonetheless have much to say about contemporary issues or the fate of a nation in times to come. Let me explore this idea by turning to a novel I wrote some years ago called *Arbella's Baby*. I was a Judge at that time, so the book was published under a *nom de plume* – Margaret Martin – with a view to avoiding controversy.

The novel is set in the reigns of Queen Elizabeth I and her successor in 1603 the Scottish king, James I, son of Mary Queen of Scots. The murder mystery at the centre of the story is gradually unravelled by the famous essayist and jurist, Sir Francis Bacon – a former legal adviser to both monarchs – and by his youthful companion, Thomas Hobbes. The reader is led to believe that what Hobbes learnt in Bacon's company affected what he said later about governance in the aftermath of the Civil War.

The story opens in London:

This in Exodus: 'Thou shalt not suffer a witch to live.' Such a text was an article of faith in England once, for without a witch to work his venom that old serpent Satan was bound to languish in his sulphur pit, a scourge to none but himself. But with the aid of an ally, so it was held, he was ever amongst us, sowing iniquities, harvesting common folk to his cause.

You must dwell upon these old times and practices as I, Thomas Hobbes, after many years in exile, acquaint you with a mystery that bedevilled my youth and came close to breaking my spirit: a puzzle that came upon me in this way.

It was customary upon the Feast of St Bartholemew to erect tents upon the green at Clerkenwell for sports and pastimes – wrestling, juggling, archery, and more. Here, the bailiffs, sergeants, yeomen, porters of the King's beam and others of prowess would challenge all men in the suburbs to wrestling matches and on the vacant ground nearby to shoot the standard arrow and compete for prizes.

And so it was, on such an afternoon, that one custom intersected with another. For stewards of the shooting match, in search of targets, had gone off to commandeer tubs and barrels from adjoining houses. Imagine, then, their panic, the horror of it, after struggling to upend a water-butt, when a dead woman, half-naked, was suddenly glimpsed and came tumbling out. At them like a thing possessed, they said. Out of the barrel in a rush, all legs and feet, and finished up flopping on the ground before them. There in a puddle, in the silent courtyard.

She was known to her neighbours, of course, the dead one, and known principally for this: she was Ellen Courtney and not so long ago had been a maid to the Lady Arbella Stuart, that notorious lady of royal blood in the house of Tudor, a claimant to the throne! But news of the dead maid's identity was quickly overtaken by the murmuring that arose. For the victim's arms were bound across her chest. The bruises below suggested that a rope had been tied around her middle.

'Afore she was hidden,' one of the archers surmised, glancing fearfully at the faces around him. 'She been dunked in a pond for a witch!'

'Aye', another whispered. 'For to see if she sink or swim.'

An investigation into the death is set in motion by the local Sheriff and his powerful superior, the Clerk of Appearances from the Court of Star Chamber, a forum renowned for its iniquitous procedures. The Clerk calls upon Sir Francis Bacon and Thomas Hobbes to assist. We learn that Bacon is keen to assist because he has fallen out of favour with King James for taking bribes while serving as a judge. Bacon foresees that the investigation will be a way of regaining his former prestige because there are certain features of the case which seem to suggest that a conspiracy is afoot to overthrow the King.

A manuscript found at the lodgings of the dead

maid, Ellen Courtney, establishes that at the time the childless Queen Elizabeth died there were two potential successors to the English throne with connections to the Tudor line – James I of Scotland and Arbella Stuart. The latter, a niece of Mary Queen of Scots, had the advantage of being born in England.

It emerges that some years before the story opens Arbella, the unsuccessful claimant, was condemned to the Tower of London by James I where she died. But it seems from the mysterious Courtney manuscript that Arbella may have had a baby – hence the novel's title – who is now a grown man. He could be planning to overthrow King James and seize the throne that his mother should have had.

In looking at the possibility of a conspiracy against King James the ambitious Sir Francis Bacon gives particular weight to a scrap of verse in the manuscript which appears to have been written by Arbella, because it points to the old law which favours a claimant to the throne who was born in England: *Look for this upon my heart, / Old Law is lost in woman's art, / Discover this upon my breath, / My claim at birth I won in death.*

For present purposes, I will skip over the various twists and turns of the plot as the investigation proceeds, save only to say that the mysterious and apparently seditious Courtney manuscript found at the victim's lodging contains clues affecting the course of the investigation and the eventual outcome.

It is said in the manuscript (at p74 of the novel):

Pamphleteers were alert to what was happening. Conversant with the reasoning of Machiavelli in his Discourses on Livy, and the precepts of Bacon in his essay on Sedition, the scribes of London were hinting in their crudely-printed broadsheets that when discords are proclaimed openly it is a clear sign that respect for government is lost. Anarchy would ensue unless reforms were undertaken promptly to remove the cause of discontent, or the ruler's principal opponent was removed by resolute action.

There is a further passage to this effect (p. 122):

Perpetuity by generation is common to beasts, according to the famous essayist Sir Francis Bacon, but memory, merit and noble works are proper to mankind. And surely we can see that some of the most striking works have proceeded from childless men and women who have sought to express the images of their minds where those of their bodies have failed. So the care of posterity is most in them that have no posterity of their own flesh and blood, for even unwanted babies, though they greatly increase the cares of life, represent the future and mitigate the remembrance of death.

It should not be thought surprising, then, in the case of a childless Queen, that in the aftermath of her death discord of the usual kind should centre not upon the absent issue of her body but be expressed in essays, tracts and images: the products of ingenious minds.

And so, let it be noted, that within three days of the Queen's passing, officials of the High Court of Star Chamber were obliged to suppress a scurrilous broadsheet being passed from hand to hand in the ale-houses of the East End, along the docks, and carried onwards by talkative boatmen on the Thames. In form, a crudely-printed publication attributed to 'A Lady's Maid', bearing the facetious title 'The Lady Arbella Stuart's Lament'; in its implications – a refrain that was bound to resonate in years to come.

The broadsheet presented to its readers, in miniature, an obscene sketch of a young male in a state of arousal, to illustrate a bawdy piece of verse: 'Sing we and chant it / While love doth grant it, / Made long, youth's part,/ Upraised by woman's art./ Now is best leisure / To take our pleasure./ the issue of his seed,/ Will meet our need.

I mentioned earlier that the investigation was set in motion by the Clerk of Appearances, a powerful official attached to the Court of Star Chamber, renowned for its draconian practices. It emerges eventually (from the various twists and turns of the plot) that the Machiavellian Clerk may have skilfully undermined the Bacon/Hobbes inquiry by planting the Courtney manuscript at the murder scene. A conspiracy is afoot but – contrary to Bacon's initial and somewhat hasty surmise – not necessarily against the King.

The scene is set for some further revelations (at p256) when the daughter of Old Bess, the Countess of Shrewsbury, says this to Thomas Hobbes about his mentor, Sir Francis Bacon:

"He betrayed the Earl of Essex. He took steps to ensure Sir Walter Raleigh was beheaded. He abandoned Lady Hatton. He prosecuted Coke. Arbella went mad in the Tower while he was Attorney General. He condemned and humiliated me. To many people at Court, he is simply a catch fart behind the throne

who will stop at nothing to serve his own ambition, which is why so many people are inclined to hate him. ... A former Lord Chancellor, you say! Look at the facts of his downfall eighteen months ago. At the height of his influence, he is accused of taking bribes. Were they large amounts to meet pressing debts? No. Far from it. ... On some occasions, it seems, he took bribes on both sides of the case. And then, having been bribed, he failed to deliver."

She gave a hideous laugh. "The chicanery of it! The effrontery! Did he offer an explanation when accused? Was he willing to defend himself? No. A quick, insincere confession, followed by a speedy resignation to abate the harshness of the penalty. Why so? To appease the King. Because he could see a chance to reinstate himself when the dust settled. Ponder his servile plea to the incumbent! Those of us who hold him in contempt have it by heart. 'I have been ever your man, your Majesty, and always but a lessee of myself, the property in me being yours.' I have it on good authority that even the Clerk of Appearances was disgusted by this abject crawling."

The Countess used her hand to scribble madly in the air. "Read your manuscript! You will see your own fate mirrored in its pages, and the fate of the mirror-maker. We are speaking of death, and death's appearance, line by line. Till the end comes, as it comes to us all."

A little later the youthful Thomas Hobbes stands by within the Star Chamber as the Clerk of Appearances and Sir Francis Bacon confront each other. Now, at last, the real issues emerge, as Bacon realises that he is the victim of the Clerk's entrapment and berates his adversary (p281):

"There is one thing sticking out of this like an ugly wart – me and my companion, Mr Hobbes, have been hoodwinked. Utterly deceived. Told lies by you about the order of events. It was you who told us that Ellen Courtney's body was discovered first. You led us to believe that some sinister plan might still be unfolding, and the subsequent discovery of Miller's body, supposedly, seemed to corroborate your reckoning. To all of this you added talk of miniatures and manuscripts that seemed to link the killings to the Lady Arbella Stuart and her circle of friends, and thus to a potential conspiracy against the crown. You spoke of a landlady observing signs of agitation when a package was received at Courtney's lodgings. And you put together a similar pack of lies concerning Miller, when clearly, it now appears, all of this was false, contrived by you to lead us astray. What explanation can you give for all of this? Do I take it that you yourself are the author of the insidious manuscripts that have bedevilled us in recent days?"

The Clerk leaned forward, and answered calmly. "I am that author."

The two men, with the narrator, Thomas Hobbes still looking on, lock horns:

Now, at last, the grim reality of what he was hearing seemed to settle upon my Lordship's shoulders. "You are against me," Sir Francis breathed. "You are totally against me, and have been committed to that course for more than a year. Longer, perhaps. How can this be? Is Coke behind it? Have you joined my enemies?"

The Clerk would make no such admission. "I am my own man," he said. "As you have always urged me to be. I am standing up for what is best."

"And what is that, pray? This 'best' you mention."

"You are unfit for office. I am the only one, it seems, with sufficient skill and subtlety to make you heed that lesson."

"You are referring to the charges of corruption brought against me?"

The Clerk nodded. "Precisely."

"The matter has been dealt with. I confessed my fault. I explained that, like so many, I was frail, and partook of the abuse of the times. A form of misconduct condoned by many others, I remind you. I was fined forty thousand pounds. Put in prison briefly. Denied the right to come here to Westminster. It is over and done with."

The Clerk shook his head sadly. "It is not over. No. You observed the usual proprieties, and acted out the posture of contrition. But without truly and inwardly acknowledging your guilt. You, a master essayist, a famous jurist, who has written so sagely about the need for integrity in judges, have sought to gloss over and excuse yourself from your own precepts – as though the elegance of your expression matters more than the substance. And now, after a very brief respite, as I knew you would, you seek to return to the scene of your pickings – unrepentant, ready to start again."

The Clerk picked up a page that had been lying on the table at his elbow. "I will quote from your letter of resignation to the King. You said this: 'I have been ever your man, your Majesty, and always but a lessee of myself, the property in myself being yours'".

With a weary gesture, the Clerk returned the sheet of paper to its place on the table. "Is that a letter for a judge to write? Surely not. If the illustrious Lord Bacon, Keeper of the Great Seal, cannot grasp the import of conventional punishment, and discover in himself a sense of shame, others must impose the lesson. If he, of all people, seems to have a blankness in him at the core, a blankness brought about, no doubt, by too much abstract thinking, by allowing the generalisations you call your thoughts to venture forth in all directions without an anchorage, the blankness will have to be written upon in the only way Lord Bacon understands – by making the reasons for his fall quite plain to him."

The Clerk then goes further and says this (p286):

"Sir Edward Coke, for all his faults, has stood up many times against the King to ensure that laws are not bent by servility or too much special pleading. He is now a worthy guardian of the people's rights. You are none. And thus I am here to condemn you. Not from enmity, although I have been shamed in your presence, but in defence of what is right. Your name that was once a whetstone in the courts to sharpen the sword of justice will sharpen nothing now."

Sir Francis shifted in his seat, seeming to sit up straighter, as he was wont to do when he saw an opening. Unwisely, the Clerk had moved the battle to a larger field, the realm of general jurisprudence, this being familiar ground to the disgraced Lord Chancellor. A place of strength.

"Pause a little," Sir Francis remarked. "You seem to accept that rights can be wrested from rulers not only by force but also by entreaty. What does that suggest? Each era calls for a different cure. My father's style as Lord Keeper in the Tudor age may not suit our present time when a Stuart king is lolling on the throne. To my mind, we are camped at a crossroads marked by chaos and increasing instability. To keep the road open, the unruly in their place, advisers with finesse and flexibility are now required. Do you want a counsellor to be so good that he is good for nothing? It is not possible to join the wisdom of the serpent with the innocence of the dove, except that men be perfectly acquainted with the nature of evil itself. Without such knowledge a virtuous adviser can do no good upon those that are wicked, to correct and reclaim them. And thus I am not abashed to be acquainted with the ways of men and women, and all their foibles."

He smiled calmly. "We must be conscious of an ever-present hunger for self-interest in ourselves and learn to adjust it to the public good. How is all this to be effected? It is best that men in their innovations follow the example which proceeds quietly, by degrees, and is scarcely perceived. And thus, he who insists upon changes or the grant of some new right, and wants the innovations to be acceptable, will be well-advised to retain the shadow of ancient rights and customs, so that the rules applied by courts and clerks appear the same, as if not altered. People are usually more affected by what a thing appears to be than what it is, and they *are inclined to act accordingly."*

Sir Francis rose to his feet, and with a mocking glance bowed to his accuser. "One can stand upon a platform, proclaim the people's rights, and beat a drum. Is that enough? Salus populi suprema lex. The overriding law is the will of the people. Let no man weakly conceive that just laws and policies designed to respond to changing times have any antipathy; for they are like the spirits and sinews, that one moves with the other. Let courts remember also that Solomon's throne was supported by lions on both sides. Let judges be lions, but yet lions under the throne; being circumspect that they do not check or oppose any points of sovereignty. For a ruler without authority will rule in the grave, and a state without cohesion will sink into a similar hole."

He placed both hands upon the table and leaned in to face the Clerk. "You have had your way. I am defeated. I accept your verdict. But I notice in your censure an over-zealous tone, a kind of fanaticism, which to me spells danger. Rights and liberties are worthless if the body housing them is swept away, and that will happen if innovations are effected helter skelter, without room for compromise, without finesse. Let me say it plainly. Without my counsel at his elbow, this King will overreach himself and refuse to accept the changes that are necessary. The unresolved points of friction will fester and weaken the authority of the state; whereupon there will be a civil war. In that, the monarch of the day is bound to be executed, and blood will be shed throughout the land. This will be paid for by those you claim to represent – the people. And at the end of it all, after the madness has abated, a monarch will be brought back to the throne for stability's sake, in accordance with our ancient customs."

He stood upright and with a movement of his hand encouraged me to join him. "You have called this a court," he said, speaking directly to the Clerk. "No matter what you call it, I stand more for the people's liberties than does your court. My faults are human. If an heir to the throne, the Lady Arbella Stuart, and a former Keeper of the Great Seal, Sir Francis Bacon, can be condemned at will. If they can have their reputations ruined in a court like this, laid low by the poisonous pen of a Clerk whose specialty is dealing in appearances: what ordinary man or woman is safe?"

At which, he turned and spoke to me before departing. "Where do you stand on this?" he asked. "Are you with me?"

In a final chapter of the novel Thomas Hobbes sets out where he came to rest in answer to his mentor's question (p293):

Certainly, we shall never know what might have happened if Sir Francis Bacon had been restored to favour with James I, and provided the crown with skilled advice as to how he should handle his increasingly fractious parliament. The punishment imposed by the Clerk of Appearances was entirely successful. Sir Francis spent the remainder of his life in obscurity; writing busily; pursuing his researches.

From birth, and ever afterwards, he had an incomparable capacity to make sense of and find a way through every ambiguity, legal and political. He was ingenious. He was eloquent. He had the ability to sum up in pithy aphorisms complex thoughts. When it came to what it was wise and fitting for the King to do, he was for the most part right. He foresaw the coming of the civil war, and tried to avert it.

And yet, there was something in the sophistry of his reasoning which eventually rendered him ambiguous within himself, and prone to shameful actions. In the meantime, and in the years that followed his downfall, his less urbane rival, Sir Edward Coke, grew in stature. By the time Coke died, his stand for the independence of the judiciary and the rule of law had made him famous among his contemporaries.

For myself, however, I have always been wary of applauding those who are generally applauded, for widespread acclamation usually means that the beneficiary is granted a special kind of prosperity by public opinion, and grows fat and self-centred. I prefer the insights of my mentor, his grit. Perhaps it was this kind of sceptical wisdom which drew me to him in the first place, and kept me faithful to him in his darkest days.

Thomas Hobbes (in the novel) noted that for all his faults, Bacon was far-sighted in foreseeing the approach of civil war and Cromwellian rule. He tried to avert it. Hobbes himself, in actuality – as a matter of real history – sought to bring his political philosophy to the English audience with the publication of *Leviathan* in 1651. This was to be his most powerful restatement of government grounded not on superstitious or religious doctrines, such as the divine right of kings (as expounded by King James I), but upon a pragmatic compact between the people who were ruled and a sovereign authority that would protect the citizenry and secure the peace – a precursor of the modern state.

Attentive readers will discern that in certain places,

in order to reflect their reasoning, I have drawn directly upon the writings of both Hobbes and Bacon. With touchstones in reality of that kind before me, let me close by quoting from John Aubrey's account of the relationship in *Brief Lives*: *'The Lord Chancellor Lord Bacon loved to converse with Mr Hobbes. His lordship was a very contemplative person, and was wont to contemplate in his delicious walks at Gorhambury, and to dictate to the gentlemen that attended him with ink and paper, ready to set down at once his thoughts. His lordship would often say that he better liked Mr Hobbes taking his thoughts than any of the others, because Hobbes understood what he wrote.'*

A novel can point the way to understanding, but in the end, if the interest of a reader is aroused by what is suggested, one must turn to legal texts and well-researched works of history for the proper story.

4

CERVANTES IN LAW

The history of a community will often include an account of controversial court cases that have arisen in earlier days, especially when a judgment based on local misadventures is handed down by the highest court in the land. If the people involved in the case seem larger-than-life, the twists and turns in the affair are compelling and the litigation runs on for years, the human story at the heart of the dispute is bound to be long-remembered.

Debated fiercely, at first by lawyers, then by others with an interest in the outcome, the story may eventually be passed on to a much wider circle as an example of what can happen if things go wrong, the perils inherent in the search for relief, the fate of parties with unreal expectations, the reward for those who refuse to admit defeat. The tale may even be handed down to the next generation of lawyers and litigants as a cautionary but inspiring legal saga, a quest for justice with the qualities of a fable or enduring myth.

In *Nagle's case* (1993) 177 CLR 423, a bathing place on Rottnest Island known as 'the Basin' was the scene of a diving accident that took the aggrieved party all the way to the High Court of Australia. The Court held that the custodian of a pool is obliged to warn swimmers about the presence of submerged rocks. The case became an important precedent. The human story is memorable also. The claimant in that case, reduced to a quadriplegic after diving into a shallow pool as a carefree youth, battled his way through various courts in what must have seemed like a never-ending saga. But the claimant and his advisers wouldn't give up, until, in the end, he was awarded $2 million in damages, 16 years after his initial, life-changing plunge.

Cervantes, a township lying between Perth and Geraldton on the West Australian coast, closely connected to the fishing industry, provides another example of a quest for justice driven by tenacity. The submerged hazard on this occasion was the handiwork of a real estate agent who became confused as to which party to a transaction he was supposed to be looking after.

The name of the township where the dispute arose is derived from that of the Spanish writer, Miguel de Cervantes, author of the famous novel, *Don Quixote*. I will have more to say about this literary link to the estate agent's handiwork a little later. But first, it will be useful to take a closer look at the activities of the agent in question who, unwittingly, brought Cervantes to the attention of lawyers on the West Coast and eventually to the legal profession throughout Australia.

The story began in this way. In 1979 Mr and Mrs Bahr acquired Cervantes Lot 221 and the business of a General Store conducted on it. Also, they had a right to call for a Crown Grant after erecting commercial premises on Lot 340. To finance the building costs of the proposed premises their agent persuaded them to enter a so-called 'sale, lease and buy-back' arrangement with one of the real estate agent's other clients, Marcus Nicolay, a small investor who was employed as an airline pilot.

The idea was that upon the land being sold to Nicolay the Bahrs would occupy the site and use the price obtained from the sale to complete their building work. They would pay rent to Nicolay as a return on his investment while the work was being done. In due course Nicolay would transfer the land back to the Bahrs at a previously agreed price.

The building was completed and the Bahrs began to operate the business as a General Store, Post Office and Newsagency, together with a Liquor Store on Lot 221. Along the way the Post Office and Newsagency business was sold to another party. But then, because some rental payments to Nicolay were overdue, the agent formed the view that the Bahrs might not be able to complete the buy-back agreement. To quote from evidence given by the agent at trial: *'At that stage our loyalty shifted from one*

*t'other, and mainly to Nicolay. The remedy was to get him out
of it in the best way possible which was to sell the property – Lot
340.'*

So the agent drew up a second contract under which
Nicolay sold the property to a local couple, well-known
in the fishing industry, Mr and Mrs Thompson. This was
arguably a breach of Nicolay's original contract with the
Bahrs but fortunately for Nicolay (and fortunately for
the Bahrs) Nicolay's solicitor insisted that the second
contract include a special clause 4 whereby the purchasers
(the Thompsons) 'acknowledged' the original contract
entered into by the Bahrs and Nicolay.

The land was then transferred to the Thompsons
under the Transfer of Land Act but without the
Bahrs' interest in the property being mentioned on the
registered title. The general rule is, of course, that a
proprietor holds the land free of all other claims save
for registered interests noted on the title such as a
mortgage, or an easement, or an interest protected by
caveat (such as an interest under a contract).

When the Bahrs sought to complete the original 'buy-
back' arrangement by calling on the Thompsons (now
standing in place of Nicolay) to transfer the land to them,
the Thompsons resisted. They did so in the belief that
the original agreement had fallen away. This belief was
brought about by the agent's misunderstanding of the
Bahrs' legal and financial position, a misunderstanding
that led to his somewhat careless advice as to what the
Thompsons should do.

The Bahrs sought relief by commencing civil proceedings in the Supreme Court of Western Australia against Nicolay, the Thompsons and the agent. The Bahrs claim, and the various cross claims between the three defendants, raised a host of issues. For present purposes, and for non-lawyers, I will do my best to simplify the matters in dispute.

There were three problematic issues standing in the way of the Bahrs' suit for specific performance; that is, their claim to the land under the original Bahr/Nicolay buy-back agreement.

First, a contractual issue: the Bahrs were seeking to enforce the original buy-back agreement but as the Thompsons weren't actually a party to that agreement it was questionable, under the rule concerning privity of contract, whether the Thompsons could be compelled to hand over the land.

The only way around the privity of contract rule was to persuade the Court that the Bahrs had an enforceable interest in the land by way of a constructive trust. In other words, as the Thompsons had 'acknowledged' the existence of the original Bahr/Nicolay contract in clause 4 of the later Nicolay/Thompson agreement, it was arguably unconscionable for the Thompsons to keep the land. In such a case, under equitable rules, the Court might be willing to find that the land was held in trust for the Bahrs, subject to payment of the previously agreed price.

But this would still leave another significant matter

standing in the Bahrs' way. This, the second issue, can be shortly described as the unregistered interest in land issue.

Even if the Court could be persuaded that the land was held in trust for the Bahrs, their interest in the land under that trust would be an unregistered interest. The basic rule under the West Australian Transfer of Land Act is that registered proprietors (in this case the Thompsons) hold the land free of any unregistered interest unless the interest in question is protected by a caveat. It turned out that the Bahrs had failed to lodge a caveat. In the absence of a caveat, the transfer of the land by Nicolay to the Thompsons arguably had the effect of extinguishing the Bahrs unregistered interest.

The answer to this second or unregistered interest issue was to rely upon one of the statutory exceptions to the basic rule. Under this exception, the plaintiffs would obtain relief if they could point to unconscionable conduct amounting to fraud by the Thompsons, the parties who were by now the registered proprietors of the land.

The Bahrs could also, as an alternative plea, fall back on a similar exception that had been approved in previously decided cases in common law. These cases allowed for enforcement of a claim in equity where the registered proprietor was held to have acted unconscionably because he or she had sought to avoid a personal undertaking. In the circumstances of the present case, the Bahrs could argue that the Thompsons not only knew about the earlier unregistered interest but also, in clause 4 of the later agreement, had expressly 'acknowledged' the original Bahr/ Nicolay contract. In other words, the Bahrs could say that the Thompsons would be acting unconscionably if they sought to avoid the personal commitment implicit in clause 4, namely, that they would honour the original Bahr/Nicolay contract whereby the Bahrs were to buy-back the subject land.

All of this, inevitably, led to considerable debate about the meaning of the term 'fraud' and whether, in the Transfer of Land Act, that term was broad enough to include self-interested but not necessarily deceitful conduct.

At the trial before a single judge of the Supreme Court the complexities of the Bahrs' case were such that the judge dismissed their claim. It addition to the two problematic issues weighing against the Bahrs' claim just mentioned, it emerged from evidence given at the trial that there was a third obstacle standing in the Bahrs' way. There was scant evidence of the ability of the Bahrs to pay the purchase price of the land under the original buy-back contract.

The usual rule is, of course, that a claim for specific performance can only be enforced if the claimants can pay the price. More particularly, as a procedural element of the usual rule, such a claim can only be enforced by would-be purchasers if they have pleaded that they were 'ready, willing and able' to complete the purchase and they have sufficient evidence to establish their plea.

It was principally this third problematic issue that led to the Bahrs' claim being dismissed by the Trial Judge. He reviewed the common law precedents bearing upon this point and, in the end, relied on a dictum of Justice Windeyer in the High Court decision of *Mehmet v Benson* (1965) 113 CLR at p314 to justify dismissal of the claim. The Trial Judge held that in the absence of an explicit plea in the plaintiffs' statement of claim that they were 'ready, willing and able' to complete the purchase and, further, in the absence of sufficient evidence to establish such a plea, specific performance in favour of the Bahrs could not be ordered.

The Bahrs wouldn't give up. They took the verdict of the Trial Judge on appeal to three judges of the Full Court, but to no avail. Their claim was dismissed again. But still they wouldn't give up. After further legal advice, they applied for special leave to appeal to the High Court.

The legal fees on all sides were steadily increasing which added an extra layer of risk to the litigation. In response to the application for special leave, like knights of old, the opposing parties buckled on their suits of armour once more, polished their shields and lances and rode into the lists for some procedural jousting. Thus, before the application for special leave could be heard by the High Court, the solicitors for Nicolay applied for security for costs; that is, they sought a court order that the losing party would guarantee payment of the legal costs of the winning party if the appeal to the High Court failed.

If Nicolay's application for security for costs had been successful, it would probably have put an end to the Bahrs' special leave application, as it was most unlikely that the Bahrs would have had access to sufficient funds to comply with such an order. Fortunately for the Bahrs, however, the application for security for costs, which was heard in Perth by Justice Toohey, was dismissed, essentially because the Court had no power to order security for costs on a special leave application. That decision, *Bahr v Nicolay (No 1)* (1987) 163 CLR 490, was given in Perth in 1987, close to 8 years after the original buy-back transaction.

The application for special leave to appeal could now be listed for hearing. When this preliminary but crucial procedural step in the appeal process was heard a few months later, the High Court, much to the relief of the Bahrs and their advisers, was persuaded to grant leave to appeal.

Another attempt was then made by all of the opposing parties to bring the appeal to a grinding halt. They applied for security costs again, but this time with respect to the hearing of the appeal itself, the final step in the appeal process. The impecunious Bahrs had no real prospect of providing security for costs, but this application, a further attempt to stymie the appeal, was unsuccessful also. The unusual circumstances of the case were such that the High Court was minded to hear the appeal without provision for security.

The appeal was heard eventually in Melbourne by a full High Court bench consisting of Chief Justice Mason and four of his judicial brethren: Justices Wilson, Brennan, Dawson and Toohey. In due course, after a period of deliberation, a decisive ruling in favour of the Bahrs was handed down in June 1988. Put simply, as to the first two problematic issues – the contractual issue and the unregistered interest issue – the High Court ruled that the Thompsons had acted unconscionably in failing to honour their 'acknowledgment' of the original Bahr/Nicolay buy-back contract and therefore held the land as constructive trustees for the Bahrs. They were obliged to transfer the land to the claimants subject only to a resolution of the third issue.

The High Court disposed of the third issue concerning payment of the price in this way. The Court held that although the Bahrs had failed to prove to the satisfaction of the trial judge that they were ready, willing and able to complete the purchase, the price was, in strict analysis, only payable on registration of a clear title to the land. Since the property was clearly worth much more than the agreed price (for otherwise there would not have been a fiercely contested legal action) the Bahrs could probably have obtained a mortgage loan to fund the purchase. Moreover, although the evidence given at trial concerning this point was scant, it seemed from the proof available that the Bahrs had in fact made some rather loose but possibly viable arrangements for financing the transaction.

It emerged, then, that the High Court, as the final court of appeal in the Australian legal hierarchy, acting perhaps pursuant to an innate desire to arrive at a just result, was prepared to place a favourable interpretation upon the evidence given for the Bahrs at trial. The High Court was persuaded to overrule the earlier findings made by the courts below and to award the land to the Bahrs.

At the end of the day, the party principally held to be in default was the agent. He had confused the parties and had failed to exercise due care. He was held liable for the loss caused by his negligence, and ordered to pay damages.

The reasoning of the High Court, as the last word on the matters in dispute, appears in the law reports as *Bahr v Nicolay (No 2)* (1988) 164 CLR 604. The final ruling had been handed down almost 10 years after the date of the original transaction. To the parties involved, as it was in *Nagle's case* (the claim by the Rottnest diver), this decade of endeavour must have seemed like a never-ending quest for justice. But now, at long last, the Bahrs were free to unbuckle their suits of armour, lay aside their shields and lances, and resume their normal lives. The High Court ruling in the case is now frequently cited in textbooks on land law throughout Australia as an important precedent bearing upon each of the three problematic issues mentioned earlier. The precedent is a talking point in property law classes at law schools and continues to be discussed by learned jurists. The angst of the parties involved in the saga is probably not so well-known.

I can't claim to be a learned jurist but I was reminded of the Bahr case while in Cervantes to attend a conference hosted by the Cervantes Historical Society. The town has grown considerably since the time of the original transaction but the premises once in dispute are still there. The shop front stands in the quiet street, mute and inglorious, but of considerable interest to any visitor from the legal world who knows the story.

In the course of my visit to the coastal town I was reminded also that Cervantes was named after an American whaler that was wrecked on reefs nearby in 1844. That ship, it seems, was named in honour of the great Spanish writer Miguel de Cervantes, creator of the charismatic knight Don Quixote, well-known in popular folklore as the man from La Mancha who tilted at windmills in the pursuit of an impossible dream.

As I foreshadowed in earlier discussion, the Cervantes name, and some ruminations about the way in which a fiercely contested legal case can add to local history, prompted me to take another look at the famous author's novel, *Don Quixote*. It is a work of fiction, admittedly, but in dipping into it I was minded to find out whether it could be said to cast any light upon the workings of the legal system, the interaction of law and literature, the presence of art in law.

To get to grips with the narrative concocted by

Miguel de Cervantes one must begin by looking at the extraordinary life and times of the author himself. Having absconded from La Mancha after a duel in his youth, Miguel de Cervantes was wounded at the great sea battle of Lepanto against the Turks and lost the use of his left hand. Taken prisoner by pirates off the coast of Barcelona in 1575, he endured 5 years of slavery in Algiers. Upon his return from North Africa, he spent many years scratching out a living, first as petitioner at the Spanish court, then as a commissary charged with requisitioning oil and wheat for the Spanish Armada and other campaigns. After that, as a tax collector, his efforts led not to renown but to imprisonment and excommunication in the aftermath of the Spanish Inquisition. This was followed by 10 years caught up in a labyrinth of bureaucratic squabbles and a quagmire of litigation resulting from irregularities.

In his later years this soldier, gambler, and failed administrator finished up presiding over a household of precarious finances and disgruntled women: an agitated wife, two sisters, a niece and his daughter by a former lover. By the time he presented his Don Quixote manuscript to a printer in the back streets of Valladolid in the summer of 1604 his future looked bleak indeed. Then, miraculously, upon publication, his picaresque novel became an immediate best seller, with the second and final part of the story being published 10 years later. The sequel was an extension of the earlier narrative in which, in an almost post-modern way, some of Cervantes' characters read about and dwell upon their own previous mishaps and misadventures.

Even now, with the benefit of hindsight, the book's success seems highly surprising, for the story, presented in a rambling and overly discursive way, seems simplistic. Don Quixote, a bookish gentleman with little money, deluded by years of immersion in the literature of chivalry and knight errantry, sets forth from his country estate to make a name for himself with deeds of valour. He and his faithful but scarcely educated squire, Sancho Panza, are caught up in all sorts of bizarre encounters until, at last, the deluded knight recognises the unreality of his impossible dream and expires, felled by a broken heart.

Shortly before setting forth from his estate Don Quixote's motivation is described in the exuberant tone that permeates the entire story: *'His judgment being completely obscured, he was seized with one of the strangest fancies that ever entered the head of any madman; this was a belief that it behoved him, as well for the advancement of his glory as the service of his country, to become a knight-errant and traverse the world, armed and mounted in quest of adventures, and to practise all that had been performed by knights-errand, of whom he had read; redressing every species of grievance, and exposing himself to dangers which, being surmounted, might secure to him eternal glory and renown. The poor gentleman imagined himself at least crowned Emperor of Trebisond, by the valour of his arm: and thus wrapped in these agreeable delusions, and borne away by the extraordinary pleasure he found in them, he hastened to put his design into execution.'*

At a first glance, it will probably strike practising lawyers, and lay readers also, that the man from La Mancha's initial aspirations and eventual erratic saga bear little resemblance to the quests for justice originating at the Basin on Rottnest Island or at the General Store in the township of Cervantes. The goal of the claimants in these cases and the steps they took to overcome the challenges presented to them were rooted in the real world. Inevitably, descriptions of what happened along the way have to be crisp and business-like. The tone is bound to be down-to-earth, or even sombre.

Nonetheless, in each case, somewhere behind the outward appearance of the matter taken to the High Court, lies a human story, a tale of tenacity, the determination to keep going. It might strike some readers that the various legal snares, the pedantic rulings on procedural points and the problematic issues confronting the claimant – due partly to rules of court governing the dispute – affected the quest for justice in much the same way as the rules of chivalry that drove Sancho Panza and the aged Don Quixote from pillar to post. It might even be thought that there was something almost incomprehensible in the tangle of issues and legal processes involved in the Nagle and Bahr cases. That illusions nurtured but not clearly defined by the law, such as truth and justice, were simply another layer of reality. That in the end there were similarities between a journey through the legal system and Don Quixote's quest.

The book written by Cervantes is regarded as a literary masterpiece, for its human sympathy, for the range and individuality of the characters encountered, and for its innovative style and techniques – the presence of an omniscient narrator with a benign view of the aged knight's delusions (*'the poor gentleman imagined himself at least crowned Emperor of Trebisond'*) and the use of different points of view to portray the inner lives of the characters. The down-to-earth realism of Sancho Panza, matched with the strange idealism of his master, reflected a profound companionship, a mood of optimistic perseverance that readers found deeply satisfying.

In various ways the style and structure of the narrative, influenced perhaps by the variety of the author's own somewhat fantastic personal experiences, underlined the contrast between a realistic and an idealistic view of life. The story points also to a contrast between the generally accepted authority of a court of law or historian in establishing what the facts of a matter are and the oblique but often insightful assertions made by the imaginative writer, the novelist or poet who reveals truth by creating fictions that reflect reality. Such a one, in seeking to explore a character's inner life, often has much to say about human nature and the motives that may have led to the doing of one thing or another. What is said may cast light upon the operation of a controversial rule or factors present to the mind of a judge seeking to act fairly.

The question of whether historians or imaginative writers should be relied upon, who has the greater authority, is dealt with in a discussion between Don Quixote, Sancho Panza and a bachelor called Sanson, a character encountered along the way. According to Sanson: *'It is one thing to write as a poet, another as a historian. The poet can tell or sing of things not as they were but as they should have been, while the historian must write of them not as they should have been but as they were, without adding or taking anything away from the truth.'*

These words are apt. One is reminded that in many areas of inquiry, especially in the law, where findings about the truth of a matter are crucial, weight must be given to the methods of historians and jurists in sifting the evidence and establishing verifiable facts. But one is reminded also by the passage from *Don Quixote* that as to some matters of importance these methods are subject to limitations. Documents and utterances may cast some light on the inner lives and motives of people involved in the matter but what they were really thinking or feeling will always be difficult to discern. Oscillations of thought and emotion are constantly taking place as events unfold. Animosities can be revived by a gesture, admiration or loyalty by a single word.

A criminal intention is a necessary element of most offences and the assumption is that this can be inferred from what the person in question said or did at the relevant time. If an accused person should seek to cover up his or her actions by telling lies after the deed, these lies, in certain carefully defined circumstances, can be used against the accused. For example, if the court is satisfied that the only explanation for the lie is that the accused knew the truth would implicate him or her in the offence, then such a lie can be received in evidence on the basis that, by implication, it constitutes an admission against interest by the accused.

The poet or novelist has far greater freedom to explore private thoughts and trace the movement of innermost feelings. What is said and done in imaginative works must inevitably be characterised as conjecture, and thus be given less weight than verifiable facts when findings are to be made, but conjecture, or even lies, can sometimes point to certain truths or a deeper understanding of human behaviour. And in some cases, the habit of pondering what might have happened may open up fresh leads to admissible evidence. An enthralling play or movie or work of fiction may also take open-minded recipients back to actual cases or historical events which might otherwise be forgotten or never known, as a first step in mastering a topic of interest.

I have conceded that my visit to Cervantes and my consequent inclination to take another look at *Don Quixote* produced a mixed result. There appears to be only a slight resemblance between the quest of the remarkable knight and the legal sagas described in earlier discussion, a resemblance located principally in the refusal to admit defeat in each case and a degree of ambiguity as to the line between reality and illusion. But it turns out that my excursion to the coastal town, and then to my bookshelves to find a battered copy of Cervantes' book, conferred collateral benefits: a fresh encounter with a great work of art and a renewed interest in the lessons to be found in such a work and in the works of the author's contemporaries.

The years between the delivery of the first instalment of the Cervantes manuscript in 1604, and publication of the second part of the book 10 years later, is of some significance for present purposes. This was a period of Jacobean rule in England, a time when the great jurist and essayist Sir Francis Bacon was coming to prominence, a time when William Shakespeare's career as a poet and playwright was entering its final phase.

Both of these writers, like Cervantes, displayed a profound knowledge of human nature and the challenges facing adventurers, from the mishaps of private dealings to the pitfalls of public affairs. The rhetoric and soliloquies of Shakespeare's protagonists, albeit imagined characters, participants in a world of illusion, always sound persuasive. Their ruminations were undoubtedly drawn from the ebb and flow of the playwright's daily life and the vagaries of the world around him.

Many of Shakespeare's characters have much to say about the law and what they say, which is obviously rooted in the playwright's understanding of social custom and human behaviour, is not only of significance in the world of make believe but can usually be taken as a valuable commentary about the workings of the law. In *The Merchant of Venice*, for example, in the fiercely-contested trial scene, Portia supports her plea for mercy with a pithy critique of the legal system which could well be heeded by jurists of today as they review decisions handed down by the High Court. *'There is no power in Venice can alter a decree established. 'Twill be received for a precedent, and many an error by the same example, will rush into the state.'*

If it be thought, as I have suggested, that there are elements in the story of Don Quixote that can be said to resemble a venture into the modern legal system, a quest for justice that demands an ending, this can be built upon by those with an interest in such matters by turning to other works of fiction about the law, from *Bleak House* by Dickens to *Crime and Punishment* by Dostoevsky. In any event, at the very least, I must close by encouraging readers, especially students or would-be lawyers, to nurture their morale, at every stage of their careers, by keeping in mind Cervantes' account of the morning and jaunty mood when the aged knight set forth.

'As soon as these arrangements were made, he no longer deferred the execution of his project, which he hastened from a consideration of what the world suffered by his delay: so many were the grievances he intended to redress, the wrongs to rectify, errors to amend, abuses to reform, and debts to discharge! Therefore, without communicating his intentions to anybody, and

wholly unobserved, one morning before day, being one of the most sultry in the month of July, he armed himself cap-a-pie, mounted Rozinante, placed the helmet on his head, braced on his buckler, took his lance, and, through the private gate of his back yard, issued forth into the open plain, in a transport of joy to think he had met with no obstacles to the commencement of his honourable enterprise.'

5

THE ART OF RECOGNITION

Give every man thine ear, but few thy voice. This well-known piece of advice by a Shakespearean counsellor at Hamlet's court has not been heeded by those who are pressing for an Aboriginal 'voice to parliament', a proposal for constitutional change that is said to be the best way of providing for the recognition and empowerment of indigenous people.

The counsellor's advice suggests that when it comes to managing affairs one should listen to what is said in *all* corners of the state and speak carefully. Ill-chosen words may lead to friction. With a nod to the need for integrity, he adds a little later: *This above all, to thine own self be true.* That is, the speaker's voice must not seem contrived or out of character. It has to reflect his or her values. It has to be clear and authentic.

The Australian Constitution, in a clear and authentic form, enriched by democratic values, lays out a system of federal government, the relationship between the central institutions and the distribution of powers between them. Within this framework, the government of the day, elected by people in every corner of the Commonwealth, is required to attend to the immediate and long term needs of the national community. In a parliamentary democracy of this kind, with a House of Representatives where governments are formed and an upper house of review known as the Senate, how will the current 'voice to parliament' proposal be fitted in? Are those for change giving *every* man their ear, or are they listening only to the plea of a particular group? Are those for change speaking with a clear and authentic belief that the creation of a special voice is consistent with the democratic values implicit in the constitution, or is what they say clouded by emotion and self-interested rhetoric?

The 2017 Uluru Statement by indigenous leaders about recognition declared that Aboriginal and Torres Strait Islander 'tribes' were the first 'sovereign' nations of the Australian continent and adjacent islands: a vast canvas dotted with laws and customs of the various tribes. The Statement called for the establishment of 'a First Nations Voice enshrined in the Constitution'. Soon afterwards the Referendum Council appointed by the Turnbull government proposed that the Constitution be amended to provide for a representative body that gives indigenous people a voice to the federal parliament and the right to be consulted on matters that affect them.

The details of this proposal have not yet been worked out. Various commentators have suggested that in the absence of a right to veto legislation the proposed Aboriginal advisory body, the so-called special 'voice to parliament', is a comfortable fit with the structure of responsible government, although it is clear from the context that this will not be a voice for *all* citizens but a voice for a certain section of the community defined by race.

A Joint Select Committee of the federal parliament presented a report in November 2018 which seemed to accept that the special voice proposal had merit. The Committee concluded, however, that further work was required to refine the proposal before it could be usefully submitted to the Australian people as a possible amendment to the Constitution. The Committee recommended that the government initiate a process of 'co-design' with indigenous leaders as a means of achieving the voice 'that best suits the needs and aspirations of indigenous peoples.' For ease of reference, I will speak of the 'special voice' as a term for recommendations favouring the proposal provided initially by the Referendum Council and a year later by the Select Committee.

At a first glance, the special voice proposal seems quite contrary to the democratic credo underlying the system of parliamentary sovereignty mentioned earlier. The term 'sovereignty' is generally understood to mean the source of authority within a nation-state for the legitimate exercise of power. Does the term 'sovereignty' truly fit the circumstances outlined in the Uluru Statement, the description of a continent inhabited by a multiplicity of tribes, a vast mosaic supposedly governed by laws and customs equivalent to an overarching authority of the kind constituted by the federal parliament in Canberra? Or are the proponents of the special voice, in their search for empowerment, using words in an artificial way and, if so, to what end?

While pondering these questions one must keep in mind not only the contentious meaning of the term 'sovereignty' but also the reality that the Australian Constitution is enriched by conventions dating back to Magna Carta. These include the rule of law: the idea that *all* citizens, high and low, are bound by the same provisions, to be applied impartially. The special status of the individual is underlined in the Australian context by the fact that constitutional change can only be accomplished by a referendum measuring the response of individual voters throughout the land. Will considerations of this kind be affected by using words in a new way or by amendments entrenching a proposal that seems to favour the wishes of a particular racial group?

It will be useful to look briefly at some history bearing upon these issues. I will do so by drawing upon the life and times of my late father who had a lengthy involvement in Aboriginal affairs. What can be learnt from the work of policy makers and administrators in his era?

Paul Hasluck was born in Fremantle in 1905. After

winning a scholarship to Perth Modern School, he worked as a journalist on *The West Australian* newspaper and soon became interested in Aboriginal affairs. Towards the end of 1933 the State government decided to appoint H.D. Moseley, a local Magistrate, as a Royal Commissioner to investigate the social and economic conditions of Aborigines in Western Australia. On the announcement of Moseley's appointment Hasluck wrote a series of articles bearing upon the issues to be investigated which led eventually to the publication of his book *Black Australians*.

Hasluck showed that in early pronouncements the Aborigines were to have the full status and rights of British subjects, but with the spread of colonial settlement these ideals had been neglected. There had been no real policy of planning a future for the Aborigines in later years save for some attempt to protect them from some of the injurious phases of colonisation. The time was overdue to plan a future that was not based on an expectation that sooner or later they would die out. Planning could only proceed, he contended, when administrators had a deeper knowledge concerning the capability of indigenous peoples and of their living conditions.

Hasluck's coverage of the Moseley Commission drew attention to a matter frequently overlooked by would-be reformers but central to any sensible discussion concerning Aboriginal affairs. In a state the size of Western Australia there was a wide variety of conditions, from fully tribal Aborigines in the remoter parts of the Kimberley, through cattle stations where tribal life was only slightly disturbed, and into the missions, small towns and settlements in all corners of the state where significant changes were taking place including exposure to European education. There were differences between those from a traditional background and those of mixed descent, some of whom were living within urban and white communities.

It was apparent to many observers by the late 1930s that there was a need in *all* cases, as a matter of law, for observance of the early ideal, namely, that the original inhabitants should be treated as British subjects with the rights and responsibilities of citizens. But it was apparent also that daily needs might vary from one region to another. Policies and protective measures should be shaped accordingly. And yet, as it still is today, administrators and many others were accustomed to using the term 'Aboriginal' without differentiation, as if people of Aboriginal ancestry were an entirely cohesive group.

Proposals for reform were stalled by the outbreak of war. A chance encounter with a fellow journalist John Curtin (who was about to succeed Menzies as Prime Minister) led to Hasluck joining the Department of External Affairs in Canberra. After the war, as a member of the Australian Mission to the United Nations, he worked closely with Dr Evatt, but felt obliged to resign when the Labor Minister's practice of favouring certain subordinates became intolerable. Not surprisingly, Hasluck was soon persuaded to join the newly-created Liberal Party. He was elected to the federal parliament in 1949.

Drawing upon his earlier experiences in the Kimberley and at the United Nations, Hasluck spoke powerfully about the need to improve the status and the treatment of Aboriginal people. In 1951 he was appointed Minister for Territories in the Menzies government. At that time the powers concerning Aboriginal peoples were principally vested in the state governments, with the federal government being responsible for the Northern Territory. There was, of course, some resemblance between policies and practices in each state, partly referable to the concept of 'assimilation' that had been the subject of discussion before the War.

The new federal Minister quickly convened a meeting in Canberra of state ministers and senior office-bearers with a view to agreeing the case for equality, bearing in mind, due to intermarriage and movement to urban areas, that assimilation was taking place in practice, save for remote communities. After the resolution of certain differences, the Minister reported to parliament in 1961 that the policy of assimilation had been approved by the various Australian governments. It aimed at ensuring that all Aboriginals and part-Aboriginals would live as members of a single Australian community, enjoying the same rights and opportunities as other Australians, and accepting the same responsibilities.

This approach was widely accepted. At that time, with the arrival of many European migrants, the term 'assimilation' was viewed as a benign description of what seemed to be the norm – a means of living harmoniously in accordance with an Australian, and essentially egalitarian, way of life. The push for integration was driven by a feeling that Australia needed cohesion, a single clear focus of loyalty that stood above sectional or racial preoccupations. Respect for one government under the rule of law, and a body of law applying equally to all citizens, seemed essential.

Some years later, the 1967 referendum provided for an expansion of Commonwealth powers over Aboriginal affairs. This change was approved by a large majority of the Australian people. This was probably due to a belief that more should be done to help Aborigines and to redress the wrongs they had suffered. But on any view of the matter, the constitutional change did not appear to imply that there should be two systems of law in Australia or two different classes of Australian. The vote accepted the sole sovereign authority of the institutions established by the Constitution but went some way towards removing any differentiation between citizens on the ground of race.

In his biography – *Paul Hasluck: A Life* – the eminent historian Geoffrey Bolton noted that by the time the 1967 referendum was held Hasluck had left the Territories portfolio to become Minister of External Affairs. He went on, some years later, to serve as Governor-

General. However, as to Aboriginal affairs, Bolton said that Hasluck's achievements could be simply stated.

'In 1933, when Paul Hasluck first began to take a serious interest in Aboriginal issues, every Australian state and territory excluded Aboriginal people from citizenship and placed them under restrictive and frequently degrading regulations. Thirty years later, when he ended his term as federal Minister for Territories, it was uniformly accepted that the first Australians had an inherent right to citizenship, and if some were still subject to restraints and limitations, official policy should work towards eliminating those arrangements as soon as possible. Race should not be the determinant of citizenship. As activist in the 1930s and as legislator in the 1950s and early 1960s, Hasluck was a leading agent for change. The referendum of 1967 that amended the Commonwealth Constitution to accommodate this change is remembered as a symbolic moment. It could not have taken place, and would not have secured such widespread assent, but for the clearing away of much of the old legislation and the attitudes of mind that supported it. Paul Hasluck played an important and honourable part.'

In his memoir *Shades of Darkness*, written in retirement, Paul Hasluck ended his account of the earlier period and the shift to self-determination as follows: 'One immediate change in method was the sudden transference of a number of fully-assimilated persons of part-Aboriginal descent into professional

Aborigines who, with the entitlement of having one Aboriginal among four of their grandparents, became the confident authorities on "the way of their people". More seriously, another outcome was the reawakening and at times the active promotion of racial divisions and antipathies. The new policy was avoiding the fact that a return to the past is never a solution to the problems of the future.'

Hasluck added: 'Fifty years ago we saw the relationship of white and coloured as a social problem …. An earnest effort was made to change Australian neglect and indifference towards Aborigines, to improve their conditions and to raise their hopes for the future. We strove for the full recognition of their entitlements – legally as citizens, socially as fellow Australians.'

Space forbids a full review of all the factors that led eventually to a widespread disparagement of assimilation, a process of integration characterised in some quarters as an overly paternalistic approach to indigenous affairs. The new credo of self-determination was presented as a fresh start but was arguably a comparable, albeit less transparent, form of governmental supervision, with funding often controlled by bureaucratic corporate bodies or imported community advisers. The latter, in some far places, when they flew in for a day, were known as "tippin' elbow" men, because they spent most of the day looking at their wrist watches before flying out again mid-afternoon. Moreover, at a time when many people of Aboriginal descent were by now living in towns and cities, it was not clear how the new credo applied to such people. One way or another, the scene was set for the divisive debate now known as identity politics.

The jury is still out as to whether self-determination has actually improved the welfare of people in remote communities. A former community manager, Tadhgh Purtill, in his recent book *The Dystopia,* describes in graphic detail the breakdown of social control in certain Aboriginal settlements following the introduction of self-determination in the 1970s and thereafter. He points out that the unresolved tension between inclusion within and separation from mainstream society continues to be a key factor. These two alternatives are at odds with each other, and therefore counter-productive, but they are both in play in contemporary times when it comes to what happens on the ground in remote communities. This tension between the two alternatives can lead to the apparently paramount importance within some organisations of ensuring the continued flow of governmental funding, as opposed to the conclusive solution of the social problems which were used to justify the funding in the first place.

New credo or not, the world is what it is. Like others in post-modern times, people in remote communities are subject to the temptations of the era from mobile phones to video games and glossy advertisements. The preservation of culture in the self-determination era requires people to learn and conform to cultural rules, but the era's emphasis upon autonomy implies the moral primacy of communal or personal choices which can be used to defend misconduct of a non-cultural kind, such as drug-taking, alcohol abuse, or general disregard for the social mores that mainstream Australians regard as minimally acceptable regardless of cultural background.

It would be a bold person indeed who claims to have all the answers in this complex field. Progress has been made since the Second World War, but incrementally, in fits and starts. An unfortunate aspect of the ongoing debate is the way in which each generation of activists and commentators feels obliged to disparage the work of their predecessors. The fog of rhetoric spread by sanctimonious activists in contemporary times tends to obscure many previous achievements.

This brings me now to the current era and to the matters I raised in earlier discussion concerning the proposed special voice to parliament, a proposal, if approved, that would give indigenous people a newly-created constitutional right to be consulted on matters that affect them, accompanied by the creation of an advisory body or special 'voice' of some sort as a part of the parliamentary process.

In October 2017, in a joint statement with the Attorney General and Indigenous Affairs Minister, the Prime Minister at that time, Malcolm Turnbull, rejected the proposal for a special voice on the grounds that 'our democracy is built on the foundation of all Australian citizens having equal civic rights, all being able to vote for, stand for and serve in either of the two chambers of our national parliament. A constitutionally enshrined additional representative assembly for which only indigenous Australians could vote for or serve in is inconsistent with this fundamental principle.'

Reliance upon this basic point of principle was entirely consistent with the democratic credo reflected in the Constitution and the changes effected by the 1967 Referendum, changes that were in keeping with the existing parliamentary structure and the move towards general equality that had been gradually taking place throughout the country. Indeed, both then and in later years, the main thrust of debate was towards ensuring that the Constitution wasn't disfigured by provisions mentioning race.

Unfortunately, however, as appears from an editorial in *The Weekend Australian* of 28 October 2017 'the manner in which the decision emerged – a newspaper leak followed by a statement from Mr Turnbull – was inadequate. A definitive decision on such a sensitive matter warranted a parliamentary statement or a major announcement.' In dealing with the role of the special voice, the editorial said also that the issue presented to Turnbull's Liberal National Party government by the Referendum Council was confused by talk of treaties. The reality was that 'the indivisible nation of Australia could not make a treaty with itself.'

The feeling of confusion ran on. Various reports drew attention to the Prime Minister's belief that the proposal for a special voice wasn't capable of winning support at a referendum and the so-called voice, whose members would be elected by indigenous groups, would inevitably be seen as a third chamber of parliament.

The PM's point about public perceptions, of how a new body would be 'seen', raised an important issue that called for an answer by proponents of the special voice. Against a background of contentious debate as to who fell within the term 'Aboriginal', at a time when the term 'sovereignty' was being reconfigured, the advisory body would almost certainly become a lightning rod for protracted debate about a vast array of current issues. It might turn out that nearly every matter of current concern on the national agenda would be seen as having an indigenous component of some kind. The paralysis of the parliamentary process induced by endless debate about a multiplicity of issues might not amount in law to a formal power of veto within the parliamentary process, but that could well be the effect of such a debate in practical terms: in many cases the approval of the advisory body would have to be obtained before a parliamentary bill could be enacted. Approval could well be difficult to achieve in contentious cases, with or without political horse-trading or financial sweeteners.

There is room for argument about this, of course, but an answer to the PM's point – his concern that the special voice would be 'seen' as a third chamber – was never provided. Proponents of the special voice shied away from saying how the special voice would operate in practice or as to what might happen if the special voice's advice was the catalyst for a widespread political controversy. Instead, they tried another tack. They claimed that Prime Minister Turnbull had wilfully misrepresented the true position because, in the absence of a formal power to veto legislation, the indigenous voice could not truly be characterised as a third chamber of parliament. Turnbull was castigated also for supposedly basing his decision on the likelihood that the proposal would fail at a referendum. Inevitably, his critics felt obliged to mention his association with the failure of the referendum for a republic, as though this too might have prompted the PM's refusal to proceed.

It was clear to many observers as the furore ran on that Turnbull's comments about a third chamber were not directed to legal technicalities such as a formal power of veto. The crucial factor was how the special voice would be 'seen'. He was making a general point about political realities and the appearance of the newly-proposed body within the parliamentary structure. Nonetheless, the proponents of the special voice used their specious claim to propagate the misleading myth that the sole reason for rejection of the special voice proposal was because the Prime Minister had falsely characterised the body as a third chamber of parliament. Since that time sympathetic journalists and academics have been more than willing to perpetuate the myth.

With the benefit of hindsight, it now seems that Malcolm Turnbull didn't make a sufficient effort to rebut the myth and to keep the debate focused on the central and very persuasive reason for rejection he provided initially: that the proposal for a special voice to parliament based on race was contrary to the democratic credo of a constitution designed to secure the rule of law and provide equal civic rights for all. That on any view of the matter, and especially when thought is given to how the special voice would operate in the arena of daily politics, the special voice's indigenous constituency, defined by race, would obtain a privileged positon in the parliamentary process pursuant to an 'enshrined' constitutional entitlement, a right of audience not held by individual citizens or by any other section of the community.

Malcolm Turnbull appeared to lack the courage and clarity of mind to stand fast and defend his basic point. In contemporary times, in an era of identity politics and corrosive political correctness, one doesn't have to dig too deep to understand why this might be so. In these troubled times, when it comes to any matter involving race, politicians, and even citizens, have to be very cautious in what they say. If one has built a career on appearing to be up to date, in step with the times, nurturing and being nurtured by the trend setters, one has be very careful indeed, especially in the seat of Wentworth, it seems.

Virtue signalling, the need to show sympathy for indigenous causes, has become so pervasive that academics, leaders of professional bodies and even captains of industry are now scrambling to profess their affection for the special voice. BHP and Rio Tinto, it seems, will be dipping into shareholders' funds to sweeten their suit, although many people, including some of their shareholders, may find the flirtation somewhat crass. Are the mining companies aiming for concessions on native title lands by waving through a radical change to the constitution? Or are they simply going with the flow? Doing what has to be done to please politically correct observers?

In a preface to his allegorical novel *Animal Farm,* George Orwell summed up neatly. 'At any given moment there is an orthodoxy, a body of ideas which it is assumed that all right-thinking people will accept without question. It is not exactly forbidden to say this, that, or the other, but it is "not done" to say it, just as in mid-Victorian times it was "not done" to mention trousers in the presence of a lady. Anyone who challenges the prevailing orthodoxy finds himself silenced with surprising effectiveness.'

Orwell went on to say: 'If the intellectual liberty which, without a doubt, has been one of the distinguishing marks of western civilisation means anything at all, it means that everyone shall have the right to say and to print what he believes to be the truth, provided only that it does not harm the rest of the community in some quite unmistakable way.'

When Turnbull was overthrown by his party a year after his rejection of the special voice proposal there was a good deal of speculation as to why he lost the leadership. There is probably no clear answer to this question, but a factor in his downfall may have been his lack of resolution in standing up for basic principles of the kind involved in the special voice controversy. He may have been contrasted unfavourably to the much-admired inaugural leader of his party. In his 'Forgotten People' speeches, Robert Menzies emphasised, as an article of faith, the importance of upholding for all citizens the rights and responsibilities of individuals, without succumbing to the demands of sectional interests.

The pressure to conform in regard to indigenous issues, to yield to any demand that could lead to accusations of racism if refused, is now pervasive in modern day Australia. Outrage can be easily confected and accusations of racism are difficult to refute. It is apparent from the Uluru Statement itself, in which communities formerly seen as tribes are now described as First Nations, and are said to have been exercising a national sovereignty of sorts, that considerable skill has been exercised in crafting plausible narratives to underpin the matter in hand, in this case the creation of a special or privileged position in the parliamentary process. It brings to mind an aphorism coined by that famous parliamentarian Edmund Burke: 'Between craft and credulity the voice of reason is stifled.'

If a Prime Minister can be stifled, shamed into silence by a prevailing orthodoxy, then it will be difficult indeed for an ordinary citizen to test the case for a special voice by asking some pertinent questions, about the adverse effect of the proposal on the structure of government, and about the way it will work in practice. If approved, the likelihood is that many members of the indigenous advisory body will feel obliged to conform to whatever is the current orthodoxy favoured by their leaders, from demands for treaties to claims for ownership or actual sovereignty over portions of the continent. They will, in any event, be focused upon outcomes that suit their indigenous constituency, because that is the purpose of the body. They will not feel obliged to give every man their ear before speaking with their special voice, or to look closely at what is best for the country as a whole. The Select Committee has said, quite plainly, that it wants a voice 'that best suits the needs and aspirations of indigenous people.'

I noted in earlier discussion that the obverse side of individual rights is individual responsibilities. This means, of course, that when an attempt is made to vest special entitlements in a particular group, the nature of the group's responsibilities will be problematic, especially when the group is diverse, ranging in this case from people living in remote communities with limited resources to people of Aboriginal descent living in suburbs or working in universities. Perhaps this is why some prominent people in the field of indigenous policy in recent times have been inclined to favour policies based on identity rather than need. They haven't lived in the stark conditions that many indigenous people contend with and they tend to believe that the politics of compassion can dispense with evidence.

Unlike the 1967 Referendum, the plea for constitutional change now, in 2019, is being driven principally by sentiment and a related push for new forms of empowerment. The case for a special voice has not been fully tested by the voice of reason and is fraught with hazard. It is questionable whether constitutional changes should be used as a vehicle for social reform, especially in a field in which policies and practices are still evolving. The best way forward for Aboriginal citizens is an unresolved and vital contemporary issue, and even within indigenous communities the nature of Aboriginal identity remains in contention.

The work of the Mosely Commission in Western Australia close to a century ago confirmed that indigenous people have been subjected to severe indignities and disadvantages. Attempts have been made to ameliorate their plight but the complexities of the situation including the variety of their circumstances have meant that much remains to be done. The remedial mood has led to significant changes in governmental policies and practices, and to some extent also at the level of constitutional law, as evidenced by the decision of the High Court in *Mabo*. But a remedial mood, of itself, is not necessarily enough to justify a profound change to the structure of the parliamentary process established by the Constitution.

The Australian constitution was cast in a form

that was intended to serve the country as a whole and to endure. It was designed to resist the plasticity of transient ideas or prevailing orthodoxies. The referendum process, involving *all* voters in *every* corner of the Commonwealth, is there to ensure that proposals for change are defined exactly and, by seeking to improve the workings of government, that they will help to secure the sense of cohesion upon which a nation-state depends.

The Referendum Council and the Select Committee seek to persuade the public that with a peck of public relations and a dash of some further phrase-mongering the special voice smorgasbord will be a feast fit for a referendum. But the composition of the advisory body, the scope of its indigenous constituency and the range of matters to be referred to it remain vague. The way in which it would operate in practice has not been properly worked out. And yet, prior to any process of co-design as recommended by the Select Committee, the Morrison government in its recent budget papers set aside $7.3 million to progress a First Nations Voice to Parliament as if the myriad of prickly issues reviewed by the Select Committee are all close to being resolved. A pattern of irresolute drift towards a referendum is further evidenced in the budget papers by a contingency reserve funding item of $160 million as 'a provision for the Indigenous Recognition Referendum' in 2020-2021.

The Labor Party seems to be of the same somewhat

unclear state of mind. In the recent election campaign it committed itself to the holding of a referendum but without saying what exactly was to be decided. Its principal spokesman, Senator Dodson, who was co-chair of the Joint Select Committee, was fully aware, no doubt, that the Committee received no less than 18 different formulations of proposed amendments for possible submission to the public. None of these were endorsed by his Committee, for his colleagues were adamant that no further step should be taken until a process of 'co-design' had been completed.

In addition to its undemocratic nature, the so-called special voice will erode the federal structure established by the Constitution. For example, as to whether the special body's advice should be submitted not only to parliament but also to anyone exercising governmental power, a leading academic observed (at para 140 of the Select Committee's report) that if the federal government of the day was indifferent or hostile to the advice the special voice could then 'leverage' its relationship with any state or territory government that seemed receptive to its views, or even with local government bodies, and 'continue to advocate for indigenous interests.' On this scenario, the special voice will rally support for its advice wherever it can until the government gives way.

To throw a spanner like this into the workings of the federal system didn't seem to bother the academic in question. An ongoing crunching, grinding sound? No worries. Just another echo in the academic echo chamber, another drum roll in the post-modern pit of identity politics, as in the ABC show called 'the Drum' where the outrage of the perceiver is generally treated as more important than the reality of the event perceived.

Like Native Title, Kevin Rudd's Apology and the creation of ATSIC, the special voice won't bring closure to the indigenous quest for empowerment. In Dylan Lino's book *Constitutional Recognition,* which provides an overview of indigenous strategies since 1967, the author – a contributor to the Uluru Statement – states quite plainly: 'Indigenous constitutional recognition should be understood not as the achievement of a final postcolonial settlement but as an ongoing process of contesting and renegotiating Indigenous and settler peoples' basic political leadership.' The co-chair of the Referendum Council, Mark Leibler, has said that the indigenous voice to parliament is not 'a shield'. It is to be viewed as 'a sword.'

Sabre-rattling of this kind by proponents of the special voice isn't helpful. The verifiable reality is that the aspirations underlying the 1967 Referendum, the moves to address disadvantage and secure an authentic sense of identity for indigenous citizens, can be achieved, and are being achieved, by familiar means – legislation and improved administrative practices – within the existing constitutional framework.

It emerges from the Select Committee's report (para 62) that in contemporary times the biggest population centres for indigenous communities in Australia are not in remote regions but in western Sydney, Melbourne and Brisbane. The interplay with contemporary life has meant that Aboriginal leaders are increasingly finding their way into positions of authority: in parliament, on the bench, within the professions and on university campuses. The process of communal mingling and further power sharing is bound to continue, as will the important contribution to Australian culture of Aboriginal musicians, writers, painters and performers. It would be patronising and unworthy of any fair-minded person to think otherwise or to insist that special categories be created for Aboriginal artists.

History, including the unique indigenous history, must be respected, but it cannot be rewritten. The form of government established by the Constitution, and the laws made pursuant to it, have become a long-standing fact of life on this continent, and underlie the Australian achievement. They are a source of benefits for the entire community. Policies and related laws can be revised as circumstances may require but the Constitution, as appears from the Preamble, is based on the will of the people as a whole whom it was designed to unite and govern. It was cast in a form that allows for change but is resistant to proposals or entreaties from sectional interests. It assumes that parliamentary institutions will not act as a voice for any particular group but as a voice for all.

To sum up: the issue to be resolved is not whether the indigenous constituency should simply be given what it wants, as set out in the Uluru Statement, and as a matter of goodwill. There is far more at stake. The central issue is whether a group within the community defined by race should be given a constitutionally enshrined entitlement to participate in the parliamentary process in a way not open to other citizens.

A special voice with an advisory role defined by race is contrary to the democratic spirit of the constitution which is based on all citizens having equal democratic rights. Further, and in any event, although the special voice will not technically be a third chamber of parliament (because it will lack a formal power of veto) it will be seen as such and its presence will probably impede or at least seriously complicate the parliamentary process. This is because, as a matter of political reality, its approval will probably have to be constantly negotiated. If its advice is consistently accepted in the course of negotiations this will suggest that it has a special power or influence of some sort and that benefits can be obtained on the ground of race which may not be available to the wider community. If its advice is consistently ignored this will, understandably, not be acceptable to the indigenous community and may lead to unwanted friction also.

The special voice proposal is a divisive concept. As matters stand at present, it is certainly far too vague to be put to a referendum as a proposed amendment to the constitution. This is partly due to the legal complexities, and partly to broader concerns. The case for constitutional recognition is rooted in the unique history of indigenous people and the privations they have endured in the wake of European settlement, but weight must also be given to the ideals reflected in the Australian constitution in its present form and to the achievement facilitated by its institutions, bearing in mind that the realities of modern life and the identity of the parties to any new arrangement are not as they once were at the time of European settlement. These concerns have not yet been fully debated or the appropriate balance worked out.

A careful appreciation of the realities suggests that at a constitutional level the challenges of the future cannot be solved by a return to grievances of the past. It would be an act of folly for a government of any political persuasion to let the special voice proposal drift towards an ill-fated vote because a failure to approve would almost certainly be seized upon by activists as supposedly a sign of widespread racism. It would be used to foster turmoil and division. If the campaign for change does continue, parliamentarians and electors should heed the advice of the Shakespearean counsellor at Hamlet's court. They should be true to their own selves by speaking up and defending familiar democratic values because ill-advised changes to the Constitution will cause lasting damage.

A case for change must be presented in a clear and persuasive form. It should not be clouded by rewritten history, artificial language, current orthodoxies or confected outrage. It should be tested by rational debate in which the government gives an ear to every point of view. If Australia is to solve its differences peacefully it should stay true to what its Constitution represents: a stable framework of government within which reforms for all can be enacted, including reforms for the benefit of indigenous peoples. Thus, on this occasion, instead of standing by, people of goodwill should make their voices heard before it is too late.